M000206174

# C.O.D.E.

## *Living Healthy, Happy, and Whole Submerged in Tragedy, Trauma, and Death*

## Volume I

Anita Agers Brooks and Darren Dake

Anita Agers-Brooks and Darren Dake

Copyright © 2018  Anita Agers Brooks and Darren Dake

All rights reserved.

ISBN: 978-0692056813

# Dedication

C.O.D.E. is dedicated to those who have fallen or
stumbled, attempting to lift others up.
To those who go without sleep, so your neighbors can rest
securely.
To those who have bruised bodies, egos, and spirits, from
taking hits most of us can't imagine.
To the real-life men and women who are too often
expected to behave as if nothing hurts.
You are noticed — you are appreciated — you are making
a difference!

WE THANK YOU!

# ACKNOWLEDGMENTS

**Cover design**
Angie Parrett of By Design Media

bydesignmedia.org

**Professional Editing**
Karen Jordan

karenjordan.net

# Praise for C.O.D.E

"After reading this book and the real true-to-life scenarios, I think this is a must-read for all first responders, police, fire, paramedics, and others who work in emergency services. After being a firefighter for over forty years, I found myself relating to each and every page. Not only is this book powerfully written, but the most important part is that it gives solutions using the C.O.D.E. acronym to help combat the demons that can plague responders. This is a book you will read more than once, and you will refer to again and again!"

**—Pete Lamb, *The Firefighter Training podcast***
Retired Fire Chief and Instructor
Pete@petelamb.com
www.petelamb.com

"These accessible stories will connect with emergency responders while also offering perspective, resources, and essential reminders of how to work horrific incidents while also connecting with friends and family. This book affirms as it educates, and it might save marriages and friendships—and even some lives."

**—Katherine Ramsland**

Author of *Forensic Investigation: Methods from Experts* and *The Psychology of Death Investigations*

"C.O.D.E provides fascinating stories of extraordinary members of emergency services who witnessed traumatic events that challenged their mental health but overcame those challenges to heal themselves and inspire others. Essential reading for those in the field."

**—Dan Zupansky, *True Murder podcast***

"From dispatch, to those on the road, and to the medical examiner, a call for help can come in different forms, but the result is the same for those who respond. Eventually, it takes a toll on the soul. In reading C.O.D.E., written by Anita Agers Brooks and Darren Dake, I was sent back to my thirteen years in 9-1-1, as an on the line dispatcher and supervisor. This is a must-read for those in public safety who have experienced the worst the industry has to offer, and who are looking to rise above the pitfalls of the job, such as depression, PTSD, Compassion Fatigue and more. "

—**Ricardo Martinez II,** *Within the Trenches podcast*
Founder of the #IAM911 movement, opening the eyes of millions to what 9-1-1 dispatchers deal with daily.

"My very first case at the coroner's office still affects me to this day — just a reminder will trigger the details in my memory, as though it were yesterday. C.O.D.E. profiles the various emotions and reactions those of us who work in the field may have experienced/felt, first hand. Each chapter in the book ends with C.O.D.E. tips, which reminds us all it is OKAY and NORMAL to feel these things, we are not alone. This important body of work gives us permission to communicate our feelings and allows others to help us, as we help those whose situations we are called upon to assist/address/investigate.
This book is a much needed resource for not only all who serve, but for the families and friends of those on call. C.O.D.E. will help those who care about dispatchers, police, fire, EMS, death investigators, coroners, and others in the field better understand the emotions and effects resulting from these all-too-common scenarios. This is a must read for all!"

—**Terri Armenta**
*Forensic Science Academy*
forensicscienceacademy.org

"This text strikes so many realistic chords with me. I've lived each of the scenarios or ones similar. I too, have seen my children lying "there". PTSD IS REAL! Unfortunately, too many of us miss the signs in others or refuse to recognize them in ourselves. For those that read this very captivating book, I hope it strikes a chord. After losing too many fellow professionals, some I knew well and some I don't know at all, its clearly time to address the issues. As a member of our departments PEER team, I'm proud and privileged to say we are headed in the right direction. Thanks to each who shared a part of your journey, and thanks to you Darren and Anita, for compiling this work. I pray it saves at least one life."

**—Criminalist Todd A. Thorne**
City of Kenosha, WI Police Department Forensic Unit
*Owner Todd A. Thorne and Associates Forensic Consultants, LLC*

"Anita Agers-Brooks and Darren Dake have written a book that should be required reading for all first responders and their family members and friends. First responders, Medical Examiners, and Coroner personnel are exposed to traumatic events every day, but expected to provide high-quality and flawless service without any regard for the physical, psychological, and emotional toll it takes on them. The authors introduce the C.O.D.E. method with incredibly moving scenarios throughout the book followed by expert tips that will assist in healing from the daily trauma associated with the job and flourishing in the job and personal and professional relationships. This book and the C.O.D.E. methods will not only extend careers but will make them ones that do not negatively impact the first responders and their loved ones. This book is a must-read and will save lives."

**—Paul R. Parker III**
Medical Examiner/Coroner Manager
Author of *Lessons from a Career in Death* Series

"Through the dissection of descriptive case studies
C.O.D.E. sheds light on an overlooked but
important topic. It is an excellent resource and must-read for
anyone in the field."

**--Mercedes Fabian, PhD**
Forensic Anthropologist, Lab Director
Anthropology Department, Human Biology Division
University at Albany
mfabian@albany.edu

# Foreword

Domestic violence, car accidents, suicide, murder. . . . You read about them in your local newspaper, online and through social media. For a time after you read the article or headline, you show emotion for those who have been hurt, but you soon move on. For you, it's over. But what about those working in public safety?

Those news stories begin with, "9-1-1, what is your emergency?" From dispatch, to those on the road, and to the medical examiner, a call for help can come in different forms, but the result is the same for those who respond. Eventually, it takes a toll on the soul.

In reading C.O.D.E., written by Anita Agers Brooks and Darren Dake, I revisited my thirteen years in 9-1-1 as an on the line dispatcher and supervisor. This is a must-read for those in public safety who have experienced the worst the industry has to offer and who are looking to rise above the pitfalls such as depression, PTSD, Compassion Fatigue and more.

The stories of Caleb and Josie were all too real. Like Josie, I took a few calls when I stopped to think, *Is this someone I know?* Working in the county I grew up in, the odds were high that it was a friend or relative. In 2007, I took a call from my cousin telling me our grandmother had just passed away. My job was tough, but I loved what I did. Like Caleb and Josie, I didn't talk to anyone, and I buried my emotions.

In C.O.D.E., Brooks and Dake walk you through cases based on true events. At the end of each story, they offer tips of hope, ways to stop and analyze your situation and better communicate your feelings with loved ones, so you can heal from the trauma.

I found closure and healing through writing my 9-1-1 stories out on my blog, *The Jabber Log*, and creating, *Within the Trenches*, a podcast based on the experience of being a 9-1-1 dispatcher. Through this, I created #IAM911. A movement that gives a raw glimpse into the emotional stress that comes with each 9-1-1 call through the words of each dispatcher.

C.O.D.E. is another crucial healing resource. Those who work in emergency services, care about someone who does, or are curious about what those on the front line deal with, should read this book.

—**Ricardo Martinez II**, host and creator of the *Within the Trenches* podcast. He is currently the Director of Communications at *INdigital*, a 9-1-1 solutions company in Indiana. In August 2016, Ricardo started the #IAM911, a movement that spread from the United States to Canada, the U.K., New Zealand and Australia. It's popularity and success has brought the Thin Gold Line into the spotlight, and has opened the eyes of millions to what 9-1-1 dispatchers deal with daily.

# Introduction

At the end of our watch we are a family: Red, Blue, Gold, White, and Black. No one fights alone in emergency services, we are all family.

During my long and continuing career, I (Darren), have experienced first-hand what the pressures the job can do to a person. Long days, missed family time, thoughts and dreams that won't go away, and ongoing relentless human destruction take their toll on your soul. The more people ignore the pain and suffering, the deeper the hole in the soul grows. It is true for every emergency career function: police, paramedics, firefighter, coroners, 9-1-1 dispatchers, and anyone else working around the violence and destruction that seems to be getting worse by the day.

At the time I started my public service career, things like PTSD, compassion fatigue, and secondary traumatic stress syndrome were not words associated with Emergency Service Workers. In fact, it was taboo and rejected by the command staff. Thankfully, over the past ten years, leadership has had a mind-shift.

As a speaker and trainer for those who work in the fields of emergency services, I looked for resources that spoke directly to the issues affecting death investigators, 9-1-1 dispatchers, EMS, firefighters, law enforcement, and others. But I found little available addressing the problems realistically, and not in clinical or textbook formats. That burning need sparked this book.

My co-author, Anita Agers Brooks, a trainer and speaker for our industry, partnered with me to tell real stories about people who work this real life. We wanted to give voice to those forced to carry on every day like it's no big deal to face human suffering, tragedy, trauma, stress, and death, as if it's normal.

"Normal," for the very select few people in the world called Emergency Service Workers, is often misunderstood by those who don't see, hear, smell, taste, and touch daily trauma. This divergence taints expectations and relationships between those who live it and those they go home to.

If this is you, we hope this book will speak to you, depicted through the stories offered and through the C.O.D.E. advice you will find at the end of each chapter. We urge you to read this book as if you are peering into this world from the outside. We invite you to view the minds and lives of people affected by trauma, tragedy, and death, both directly and indirectly.

Read each section dedicated to the various branches of Emergency Services Workers, not only those directly impacting you, but also delve into the days of those you work with and around. You will learn from others, plus gain confidence that you are not alone.

If you care about someone who sacrifices body and soul for the sake of others, we hope these chapters give you eyes into the hearts, minds, and spirits of those who serve on the front line of the best and worst of human conditions. Our hope is that these stories will strengthen your relationships and enable you to connect more deeply with those you care about.

—**Darren Dake**, *Coroner Talk podcast*
Author and national speaker
Retired Military Police, retired law enforcement officer, present-day coroner
Founder of the *Death Investigator's Training Academy*
Certified instructor for the *Law Enforcement Learning Center*

\*\*\*

When I wrote *Getting Through What You Can't Get Over*, I (Anita), did not foresee the doors that would open for me to make a meaningful difference for men and women who serve on the front line of emergency services. I will always be grateful for the gift of speaking into the lives of those who protect, serve, and save.

As a Common Trauma Expert, Certified Personality Trainer, author, international speaker, and Certified Trainer for the Law Enforcement Learning Center and American Board of Medicolegal Death Investigators, (ABMDI), I am honored to help provide a resource for those who live to give. I hope all of the respect, compassion, concern, and admiration I feel for emergency services workers around the world is conveyed in the following pages. I realize you often feel undervalued and unappreciated, but it is our intention through C.O.D.E. to not only encourage you in your work, but to assure you it is noticed, and it matters — very much.

To all who sacrifice, thank you for your diligence, integrity, and dedication, making it possible for the rest of us to sleep better at night. If you haven't been told lately, or ever, the world *is* a better place because you exist.

—**Anita Agers Brooks**, *Tending Your Dreams podcast*
Award-winning author, international Speaker, and inspirational life coach
Certified personality trainer and common trauma expert
Certified instructor for *Law Enforcement Learning Center*
and *American Board of Medicolegal Death Investigators.*

# Contents

## Death Investigator Summary

Death investigators deal with the awkward, horrific, and taboo on a regular basis, yet outsiders of this field seldom consider what they do for the rest of society. Their lives are permeated by the scents and sights of bodily fluid, internal organs, blood, and brain matter. It sometimes lingers in their nostrils and memory for weeks.

These unflinching men and women are front-seat observers to the sad awakenings of people who are ripped from their seemingly normal lives, thrust into the maddening clutches of death. The unspoken is their normal. More than one death investigator has expressed their odd attraction to death, where plasma, maggots, bone fragments, trauma, and mournful screams provide a strange allure.

What most people around them don't see until the effects have magnified to the point of crippling anxiety, depression, Compassion Fatigue, and/or Post Traumatic Stress Disorder, is the accumulating impact of the job. From what we've been told, you can't plunge into the crevices of life's end and emerge unscathed. At some point, whether emotional, mental, physical, financial, or relational, there will be consequences for choosing this field, though there will undoubtedly be moments of deep satisfaction, celebration, and success that make it worthwhile.

This section is dedicated to those who dare to abandon self, for the mission of helping others come to terms with death. If you work as a death investigator and have not heard it lately, or ever — you are appreciated, your work is noticed, and people are grateful for your sacrifice. Thank you!

# Chapter 1
## Spiraling to a Crash

Remnants of death scenes were beginning to dissipate from Caleb's exhausted brain. He rubbed his right temple, unaware that his wife, Julie, watched.

Her touch on his arm startled him. "You okay?" Concern tinged Julie's tone.

Caleb pulled back as if scalded by a hot brand.

"Shutting me out isn't helping. Let me in. I love you, but if you don't tell me what you're thinking, I can't support you."

Caleb scowled at Julie. "Your pressuring isn't making anything better."

"I'm your wife, we're supposed to be in this marriage together. For better or worse. Remember?"

"Drop it."

"But I . . . ."

Caleb's open palm slammed against the table top. "I said, 'Drop it.' Now."

The coroner's ring tone on Caleb's cell caused Julie to close her mouth — freshly opened to retort. She pushed away from the table and walked out of the room, leaving Caleb to deal with whatever new case demanded his attention. On the other end of the line, Central Communications, known as Cen-Com to those who worked in emergency fields, alerted the assistant coroner that at least one person was confirmed dead in the neighboring town of Hollister. With a sigh, Caleb got up from the table and headed toward the front door. He didn't bother trying to kiss his wife goodbye.

Smoke billowed skyward as Caleb neared the crash scene. He took a deep breath to stifle his adrenalin flow while he put his black Suburban in park, then pushed the driver side door open.

Burning jet fuel singed Caleb's nostrils with the stench of destruction. He stood beside his vehicle, taking in the horrific landscape. Several feet from a patch of smoldering black grass, small plane fragments were scattered in a large circumference surrounding the impact site — accompanied by detached body parts. A muffled crackle, interspersed with the occasional pop, told Caleb that embers were still alive in the wreckage, hidden from view.

Caleb lasered his attention on as many details as he could take in from his distant vantage point. He jotted notes into his smart phone, then carefully backed out of the area. Until the Federal Aviation Administration arrived and gave him instructions, Caleb couldn't process the scene.

Was the hot air brushing Caleb's face and arms caused by the crash or mid-June, Oklahoma winds? He wasn't sure, but it was obvious he wasn't the only one affected by the vaporous heat. Major Wentzel of the sheriff's department approached from the west, swiping his forehead as he walked around the crash.

Major Wentzel rubbed his palm against his pant leg as he spoke. "The FAA investigator called and said you can start marking the evidence, but he doesn't want us to do any removal until he's on the scene."

Caleb nodded in agreement, then said, "I'll take some photos as is, then I'll flag the scene and get shots with the markers in place. How about red for plane parts, blue for the items we deem as passenger personal effects, and yellow for human remains?"

"Sounds good," Major Wentzel said. "One of our officers can assist."

"I can probably recruit someone from the fire department to help too."

"I'll leave you to it." Major Wentzel turned and walked toward his patrol car.

Moments later, spurred by the major's prompting, a deputy sheriff offered his help. Caleb placed the yellow markers and a female fire fighter set the blue identifiers near items belonging to deceased passengers, while the deputy stuck red flags near shards and shrapnel forged from the plane's explosive impact with the ground. When Caleb felt sure they had tagged all of the evidence, he took photographs from several angles around the area, then he backed out carefully to wait for the arrival of the Federal Aviation

Administration. He sat in his car with the air conditioner, his thoughts blowing full blast for nearly an hour.

Julie's words reverberated while Caleb waited. Deep in his soul, he knew his wife was right. They weren't as close as they used to be, and much of it was his fault. But how could he tell her about the kind of gore he saw every day? If she were looking through his front windshield right now, she would say the scene outside was gruesome. But Caleb didn't have the luxury of focusing on humanity — he needed to concentrate solely on the facts. His mastery of flipping that mental switch served him well on the job, however, his ability to stifle his natural human emotions was causing negative repercussions at home. Thankfully, a black, unmarked car pulled up, rescuing Caleb from his musings.

A strong blast of hot wind forced Caleb to expend extra energy to thrust his car door open. A man of medium build with cropped sandy colored hair and dark eyes stepped out of the government issued sedan. He held out a his hand, and gave Caleb a firm shake. "I'm Allen Arlie, investigator for the FAA."

Neither man smiled, not for lack of cordiality, but because the crisis called for serious professionalism.

Caleb explained the flag marking system, while Arlie nodded to affirm his understanding and approval. Caleb followed the examiner through the maze of body parts and metal shards in silence, only commenting when asked.

Arlie took his own pictures and notes methodically, only stopping after he had completed a thorough review. He stepped aside to make a brief phone call, then he turned to address Caleb and Major Wentzel, who had joined them as they assessed the last section.

"We have additional FAA personnel responding, as well as a National Transportation Safety Board investigator from Dallas. He won't arrive on scene until approximately 1730, so you can remove the remains. But please make sure all of the flags stay in place."

Wentzel added, "Tracing the aircraft serial numbers, we confirmed the plane only contained one pilot and one dog, a black Labrador Retriever. The pilot has been identified as a thirty-nine-year-old Caucasian male by the name of John Morris Ross. His flight plan indicates he was flying from Springfield, Missouri, to Lawton, Oklahoma."

Investigator Arlie nodded grimly. "Excellent work, gentlemen. The NTSB investigator will be here in a few hours. I'll move on so you can finish up."

Allen Arlie's black sedan disappeared into the distance, soon followed by the fire trucks, ambulances, and all but one deputy. Then, Caleb's boss, the Tillman County coroner, showed up. Even with his help, Caleb had hours of collection ahead him.

Prior to gathering and examining the remains, Caleb completed a sketch of the wreckage area. The assistant coroner marked the distances from known points and identified the two largest body parts as boundary limits — the smaller pieces were scattered amid the simmering wreckage. With that finished, Caleb tugged a pair of latex gloves over his hands, snapping them over his wrists.

Working side-by-side, Caleb and his supervisor carefully picked up each appendage, member, tissue, and bone, whole and mangled. They bagged and sealed each of them with a zipper lock, labeling the individual bags with number 044896. A quick inventory alerted them to a potential problem.

The coroner furrowed his brows as he spoke to Caleb. "We're missing both feet and part of the right leg." A familiar smile crept along his lips. "I guess you could say we need a leg up," the coroner cackled at his own joke.

Caleb rolled his eyes. It wasn't the first time he'd heard that line in one form or another.

Crunching gravel caused both men to look up as a beige rental car rolled to a stop near their own vehicles. A tall man got out, stood, and smoothed his khakis and polo shirt. He leaned back into the car head first, then emerged with an iPad in hand.

Caleb and the coroner simultaneously moved their bodies into a more dignified posture and walked toward the dark haired man as he approached from the opposite direction. As the three neared each other, Caleb deduced by skin tone, facial features, and eyes, that the stranger came from a Latin or middle eastern ethnic lineage. Caleb held out his hand.

The man smiled cooly. "I'm Specialist Tom Giles. NTSB. Small crash site, single engine?"

"I believe so," Caleb answered when the coroner looked to him. "The pilot and his black lab were the only passengers — both deceased."

"I never get used to death," Specialist Giles said. He sighed, "Better start while there's daylight left."

The coroner extended his hand to the NTSB specialist, "Caleb will help with anything you need. I have to get back to the office and finish my report on another case." His eyes glinted for a moment, making Caleb groan silently at what he assumed was coming. "Hopefully, Caleb can give you the leg up necessary to close the scene before dark." The coroner was still chuckling when he climbed into his SUV.

If the specialist had a clue about the nature of the coroner's humor, he didn't let on. Instead, he walked to where the bulk of the plane's core rested in the field. Caleb followed. Forty-five minutes later, digging strategically through the wreckage under the watchful eye of Specialist Giles, Caleb saw what he believed to be a pair of chewed-up shoes beneath the airplane. But he couldn't retrieve them due to the plane's position. At least not yet.

After a fitful night's sleep next to Julie, who wasn't speaking to him, Caleb left home just after dawn to return to the crash site. His suspicion about the shoes was confirmed soon after his arrival. The items were recovered after the removal crew lifted the plane, exposing the area, along with the feet and missing leg. Caleb bagged and tagged them.

Before leaving, Caleb located the dog's remains and repeated the bagging process — per the family's request. He then released all of the remains to the transport crew for examination and the collection of toxicology samples as required by the NTSB.

Seeing the final pieces of debris loaded for transport stirred mixed feelings in Caleb. Now he had to deal with his never-ending piles of administrative work in the office — the monotonous part of his job. Compared to that and what he faced at home, Caleb already missed the presence of dead bodies. At least when he was working with them, he got an adrenalin rush, without the pressure of someone trying to make him do something awkward.

### Profiling Caleb's Reactions

We often miss the danger of invisible drains in relationships. Those common, overlooked influences that can make for a good or bad day with those we share life with. In Caleb's situation, there were factors that not only impact his frame of mind, but his ability to achieve personal satisfaction and professional success.

But identifying and facing those things causing us to lose precious time, energy, money, and intimacy, can help us plug them. Caleb could have experienced greater peace, rest, prosperity, and a healthy connection, by addressing the issues disrupting his life.

### Questions to Consider

- **What would help Caleb handle his dread of paperwork?**
- **How should he best approach the current conflict at home?**
- **What is the next best step Caleb should take to regain a balanced view of the situation?**

### C.O.D.E. Conduct

**Communication** — Most professionals would never dream of refusing to communicate with their superiors or their co-workers, understanding the perils when relevant information isn't passed on. Too often however, they forget the dangers of refusing to communicate clearly with their own family members. If this goes on long enough, the individual risks losing their loved ones, and the personal fallout could destroy a career. Talking isn't always comfortable, but having appropriate conversations on a consistent basis with key individuals, can protect and save crucial relationships.

**Objectiveness** — Objectively analyze all of your relationships: office, field, and home. Are there any weak areas that need attention? What can you do to rectify and improve them?

**Dedication** — Are you dedicated? Not just to the job, but also to the people impacted by the work you do. What is your mindset toward your colleagues, family, friends, and the people you serve?

**Engagement** — Give yourself permission to connect and reconnect at appropriate times with the right people after you've had to detach to take care of business. One of the unique challenges of working in any kind of emergency services field is the necessity to block your emotions so you can get the job done. But if you don't practice intentional efforts to turn your feelings back on, it is impossible to maintain healthy relationships with spouses, children, extended family and friends.

## Chapter 2
## A Cooling Marriage

Tish knew it was wrong.

Her fingers trembled as she texted him back. *Can't wait for you to hold me in your arms.*

The screen on her phone lit up in seconds with Sean's response. *I'm on fire. Tonight can't come soon enough. What time can you get away?*

Guilt washed over Tish's soul in cold waves. *Gotta go. Meet you at Eaton's. 10:00. Unless I get called out.*

*I'm on standby too. Hoping for a quiet night. I need you.*

Heat, mixed of passion and shame flooded Tish's veins. It heightened when the front door opened, and Paul called out. "Hey babe. I'm home. What's for dinner. I'm starved."

Tish fumbled to delete the messages on her phone. She prayed her voice wouldn't tremble, giving her away. "Lasagna's in the oven," she called out to her husband. "Should be ready by the time the kids get home from their practices."

"Awesome," he walked into the kitchen just as Tish laid her cell on the counter. Paul grabbed her before she could protest. He spoke into her hair. "Hmmm, something smells good, and it's not the food."

Tish pushed off her husband's chest. "Not now."

The hurt look on Paul's face said what he didn't express with words.

Like she had a dozen times before, Tish wondered, *What did I ever see in him?* She busied herself in the fridge, pretending to pick through the vegetable bin, rolling a red pepper off of a green stalk of celery. *Life would be perfect if only Paul was out of the picture. Then Sean and I could be together — well, if that hag Sean was married to also disappeared.*

"What are you looking for in there?" Paul's physical nearness permeated Tish's fantasies.

27

She bumped her head in a rush to stand up, waving a head of lettuce like a trophy in Paul's face as she turned on him with a growl. "Can't I make a salad without your criticism?"

"What's your problem lately? Why do you keep picking fights?"

Tish stared her husband down, hoping a steely gaze would cover the intensity of her beating pulse. It seemed to work.

Wearing weariness like a cloak, Paul left the room.

A few hours later, after lying about a new case call, Tish collapsed into the safety of Sean's arms. Any thoughts of Paul or their children were quickly shoved into the furthest recesses of her mind, smothered with a heavy dose of justification. *I'm tired of coming in last, don't I deserve some happiness of my own?*

The sound of both their phones ringing simultaneously was not a welcome sound.

Thirty minutes later, Tish entered the residence of 419 Dove Street. She nodded at Deputy Kerry, who nodded back.

"Body's in there," he pointed to a doorway at the mouth of the hall.

Tish crossed the threshold, and hit a wall of smells unique to the dead, a thick blend of human vomit, feces, and other released bodily fluids. A digital camera clicked from a corner, capturing the image of a gray/blue tinted female body who appeared to be in her early to mid-thirties.

"Who found her?" Tish directed her question at the young officer standing quietly to the side.

"Husband. He said she was released from the hospital with a bad case of the flu four days ago." The officer clicked his cell phone to read from his notes. "He told me she was feeling better when she first came home, but by the next evening she was projectile vomiting, running a fever, and dripping in cold sweats. He said she drank Gatorade to try and hydrate, but had difficulty keeping it down. Said she refused to go back to the hospital."

Movement caught the corner of Tish's eye. She instinctively turned, but at the sight of Sean, dropped her eyes back to the body, hoping no one noticed the intimacy in their brief exchange.

The young officer straightened his stance as Sean fully entered the room.

Sean addressed his subordinate, as if Tish didn't exist. "What are we looking at, Stan?"

"Not sure, Chief. I was just telling the pathologist here that the husband said she'd been sick, real sick, but wouldn't go back to the hospital."

"What was his demeanor?"

Stan shifted his weight, and squinted his eyes unconsciously. "He didn't seem all that upset. The way he interviewed felt off. What really got me was when he said she acted drunk and was even crawling around the floor on all fours, but didn't take her to the hospital until one of his sons insisted. He sounded stone cold when he described it."

Sean grunted, then said, "Let's bag as much evidence as we can." He pointed to three partially empty Gatorade bottles on the night stand. "Did you ask for her cell phone?"

"Not yet. But I was getting ready to," Stan's neck turned crimson up to his ears.

Sean addressed the crime scene photographer, "Do me a favor and get a shot of every inch of this room, and make sure you capture different angles, then do the same in the kitchen, bathroom, and living area. I'm going to walk this residence, so I may want a few other shots as well."

Sean turned as if he were going to walk into the hall, but paused without making eye contact with Tish. "Ms. Hampton, please don't touch anything except the body until we are done. I have a feeling about this one, so it may take longer than usual for us to release the remains to the medical examiner's office."

"Of course." Tish's words were wasted on Sean's disappearing back. Though she knew his detached demeanor toward her was necessary, she still felt an emotional sting. Tish tried to assure herself. *Don't make it personal. He can't let anyone know about us, so he has to play it cool.* But it didn't quite take away her ache.

Normally, Tish wasn't called on scene, she dealt with

the dead in the autopsy room. But the budget in their small county only allowed for the coroner and herself, and since the coroner was on vacation, and the lead homicide detective wanted a medical examiner's take on the scene, Tish handled the case from beginning to end.

Once Tish got the woman's body to the morgue and began the autopsy, she quickly discovered the reason for death. Oxalate crystals were evident in the kidney tissues she put under a microscope. The slides illuminated by polarized light microscopy revealed a Birefringent crystal content in the 3+ range.

In the coming days and weeks, as more test results came in, Tish's suspicions were confirmed. It was evident from the pathological evidence, ethylene glycol, more commonly known as the poisoning agent anti-freeze, had been introduced to the victim's body slowly with an accumulating effect. The victim would have died in an excruciating and tortuous way. Each time Tish queried about the facts uncovered during law enforcement's investigation, the answers sent chills running down her spine.

For months, Sean and his team quietly unraveled the threads connecting the case. The details made Tish more and more uncomfortable. In the privacy of their stolen moments, Sean shared his hypothesis with Tish, saying he believed the female victim, thirty-two-year-old, Joanne Phipps, was killed by her husband, who was having an affair.

Caught up in his passionate tirade about the suspect, Sean's voice elevated as he told Tish, "Only weeks prior to her death, he had increased the value of one life insurance policy on his wife's life, and had secretly purchased another."

Increasingly, in the warmth of Sean's arms, Tish would shudder. She had told no one, not even her lover, of the many times the dark fleeting thought had crossed her mind prior to Joanne Phipps' death. Of the brief fantasies of Paul coming to an untimely demise. Of Sean's wife expiring soon after. Of collecting life insurance money, so she and her illicit lover could run away to an exotic location together. Growing guilt was making Tish more uncomfortable by the day.

About three months after Joanne Phipps' death, as she

lay spent beside Sean, the image of her children's faces flashed in Tish's mind — but this time, she did not push her thoughts away. Instead, she untangled herself from Sean's arms and crawled out of the bed.

Seconds later, Tish stood in the bathroom. Door closed. Alone.

She looked at the woman in the mirror and whispered as she bore into the horrified eyes she saw reflected there, "Who have you become? I don't know you anymore."

When Tish walked into her house an hour later, Paul looked up with surprise written on his face. "Home already? I figured it would take you longer tonight."

Tish suddenly saw her husband through a new lens. She heard the tenderness in his voice. Saw the concern etched into the furrow of his brow. Noted the tidy yet disheveled living room. She swallowed. "Are the kids in bed?"

Paul looked at his watch. "Yeah, baths and pjs almost forty minutes ago."

"Good. Can we talk?"

Paul smiled and patted the couch cushion next to him. Oblivious.

Tish barely made the four steps it took to reach him, before her knees gave way under the weight of her internal emotional pressure. She and her husband never went to bed that night.

The day after Tish confessed her adultery to Paul, she texted Sean and ended her affair. Temptation still presented itself unbidden at times, especially during the initial weeks when Paul's reaction to the betrayal brought the most heat — and when Sean's persistent messages planted doubts in her mind. But Tish refused to buckle, and chose over and over to deny the justification that wanted to add more chaos to the situation she'd already created. She continually reminded herself of her determination to learn to like the woman in the mirror again.

Eventually, Sean finally got the message and stopped reaching out.

Several months and many counseling sessions passed before Tish and Paul broke through their grief, worked through old, unresolved hurts, and learned the art of communicating clear expectations in reasonable and respectful ways. They developed new interests together, including regularly scheduled date nights and attending a local church. Slowly, their life together improved, as they learned to forgive and laugh together again.

Tish felt deep gratitude for her husband's willingness to push through the most painful period either of them had ever faced. Because he had forgiven her, she loved him even deeper. The ways they were both learning to demonstrate their love in action soon brought promised results — though not nearly as quickly as either of them would have liked.

Tish also changed jobs, moving to a location that would mean little if any interaction with Sean. Protecting her marriage, her children, and their life together became her first priority.

Sadly, Sean's marriage disintegrated when he was caught in another tryst. The last Tish had heard, his children weren't speaking to him, his divorce had cost him his home and car, and he was living on a friend's couch. A mutual friend had told her, "He's in such denial. He still blames everybody else instead of taking responsibility for his choices. I know of at least half a dozen women he slept with when he was married." Then her friend's face shaded — apparently he'd heard the departmental rumors.

Tish felt relieved she'd escaped what would certainly have been a disastrous relationship with a man like Sean. She was thankful her marriage was intact and healing, and her children still had Dad and Mom to come home to.

She was also relieved when Joanne Phipps' husband was convicted of murder. He'd planned well, but not so much that the facts didn't ultimately trap him. Both situations had taught Tish some priceless lessons.

A year after her confession, Tish took a piece of neon yellow construction paper, and in a thick black marker wrote at the top: Never Forget. Then she listed bullet points beneath.

*She/he who has nothing to hide hides nothing — especially from themselves.

*If you want a happy home life, you need to make decisions proven to produce happier outcomes.

*Invest intentional gratitude in your spouse instead of focusing on their faults.

*Avoiding your problems by running into someone else's arms doesn't solve anything, but instead, heaps new and bigger issues on top of the existing ones.

It took time, but the day came when Tish could finally look in the mirror and smile once again. The first time it happened, she knew she was free.

## Profiling Tish's Reactions

Human beings make mistakes, but like most of us, Tish tried to hide the truth beneath justifications, denial, and blame. The more committed we are to keeping secrets, the greater the damage we create. We often struggle to believe it's possible for us to cross certain lines, however, one guilty act often leads to others. A fleeting thought can transform into a dark seed, unless intentionally uprooted and removed.

Tish would have avoided a lot of pain and angst, if she had applied one of the greatest relationship protections a person can put in place. In advance of any temptation, before you are faced with a life-altering choice, decide that crossing unethical, immoral, or unloving lines is not an option. Waiting and hoping you will choose rightly in the heat of the moment jeopardizes your entire life as you know it.

## Questions to Consider

- **What would have helped Tish avoid causing herself and others this pain?**
- **How could she have stayed focus on her work while processing her emotions in this volatile situation?**
- **Where could she go for assistance in learning to forgive herself?**

33

## C.O.D.E. Conduct

**Communication** — What we say to ourselves is the first line of defense against destructive temptation. Reminding ourselves that greener grass often results from fertilizer can help. That sparkling emerald invitation in front of you, may hide a leaky septic tank beneath the surface of what you see. Ask yourself what you are trying to escape from when your emotions move you to run from reality in any way.

**Objectiveness** — If you must work a scene or case with a red flag colleague, (someone who presents a dangerous temptation), get in and out as fast as possible, keep your eyes and mind on the job at hand, and recruit help from others to reduce your exposure.

**Dedication** — Passionately dedicate yourself to focusing on the traits, talents, and treasures of your family members. When we concentrate our minds on what we are grateful for, we aren't as prone to complaints, betrayal, and destructive actions. Imagine boundaries and warning signs on your person as you work the job. Invisible lines you won't allow unhealthy relationships to breach or signs that say, "Unavailable," attached to your forehead.

**Engagement** — Protect your family by intentionally spending quality time together. Envision yourself as the champion of your family. The hero working the job for them, so you can come home guilt-free.

# Chapter 3
## Secrets of Auto Erotica

"Oh boy," Brad Cullen muttered to the dead body in front of him, as he entered the room.

A man in his mid-sixties, lay slumped in a beige recliner, wearing only red, spiked heels, a long, royal blue neck tie, and a red lace bra. His head was pulled down toward the left arm of the chair. A vacuum cleaner continued its electric hum next to the recliner. The end of the tie was wrapped around a large brick, laying on the floor by the chair. From the scuff marks on the side of the chair, it appeared as if the brick had fallen from a perch on the left armrest.

Brad could hear the man's wife screaming from the kitchen area, where police officers were trying to keep her distracted. She had found her husband's body less than an hour before. The loss was bad enough, but Brad could only imagine her shock at the state of his body when she walked into the room. Even as a seasoned death investigator, Brad felt a little weirded out himself.

"Well, you've certainly made an impression," Brad said to the cadaver. Taking a deep breath, Brad steeled himself to remove the man's penis, still inside the suctioning vacuum hose. It was apparent he'd used it as an aid to his masturbation, and by the looks of things, it wasn't the first time. But first, Brad needed to take pictures from multiple angles of the scene. This was one for the books.

After Brad finished taking the photos, and jotting down reminder notes, he unplugged the vacuum. Through the years, he'd dealt with a lot of uncomfortable situations involving the human body, but the removal from the hose ranked at the top.

From the kitchen, Brad clearly heard the widow crying. She told the officers, or maybe it was more to herself, "I don't understand. How could he do this? We've been married almost forty years, and I had no idea. I went shopping, like I do every Saturday, but when I got home, the door was locked. I was so confused. How could I not know? How is this happening?"

Shock and denial —Brad recognized the first stage of grief. And this poor woman would have a unique and bumpy road to recovery. Not many wives found their husbands dead from hidden sexual fetishes.

During autopsy, Brad discovered that the cause of death came from suffocation. The ligature marks on the man's neck, proved he'd used the neck tie to restrict the oxygen to his brain, causing a heightened sexual response. By the blood lines evident beneath the skin, the man had used a slightly downward pressure to alter his state of consciousness, a common practice among those who delved into the dangerous world of auto erotica.

Some, like the man on the table before Brad, carried it too far, and whether from a slip or something else, found it impossible for them to loosen the tension in time. The force required to bring about unconsciousness and even death, was not nearly as strong as a person might imagine. And death was never long in coming when extra seconds of asphyxiation took place.

At the death scene, Brad had noted the pornographic magazine on the man's lap. That, along with his manner of dress, the way the neck tie was used, as well as the running vacuum cleaner, made it obvious that the scene and his body pointed to a case of auto erotica death. Though the family knew nothing prior to the man's passing, his wife did note that she had seen red marks on his neck previously, after coming home from her weekly shopping trip. Her husband told her he'd simply been scratching his neck.

What wasn't at the scene spoke as much as what was. There was no suicide note or other evidence of suicidal intent. Brad also saw no proof that any others were involved with the act that caused the man's death. The auto in auto erotic meant self, or on one's own. The man had accidentally taken his own life — and in a most embarrassing way at that. Brad would not forget this particular case for a long time, and it would affect his home life in an odd way.

It happened first, three nights after Brad wrote his final report on the auto erotica file. He woke up to find his pillow wet. The dream had caused him to sweat so much, his sheets were damp. He looked over at his wife and thought, *I hope Elicia doesn't find out about this.* The clock on his nightstand read 4:12 a.m.

Brad tip-toed out of their bedroom. He fell back on the couch, and put his hands over his face. The widow's voice flashed through his mind. He whispered into his cupped hands, "How is this happening?"

The bed clothes dried before Elicia woke up, so at least that was a relief. But Brad struggled to look his wife in the eyes. Images from the dream kept flitting across his mind, making him feel even worse. Over breakfast, Elicia even caught him in a blush.

"Why is your face red, Babe?"

Brad quickly reached up and touched his right cheek. The warmth told him what he didn't want his wife to see. "I don't know. Maybe I'm running a fever."

Elicia leaned over and felt his forehead. "You don't feel hot."

Brad didn't tell his wife that the heat he felt came from an internal source. Humiliation.

Never before had a death investigation done this kind of thing to him. Brad's dream had awakened him due to its vivid nature. In it, Brad was the one in the beige recliner, sprawled out in women's lingerie with a household cleaning device attached.

It was his body's response to sexual arousal that woke him up, and threw him into an emotional tailspin. But the effect on him didn't end there. A week later, he was still trying to squelch the memories of the nightmare. On Monday morning, he looked in the mirror while getting ready for work. Early again, after another disturbing dream. *With all of my training, my clinical knowledge of the human body, and my understanding of how the brain is wired, why can't I turn these thoughts off?*

Elicia came up behind him and wrapped her arms around his waist. She nuzzled his ear in a suggestive move, but with fresh embarrassment on his mind, Brad twisted and slipped out of her embrace.

"Hey! Where are you going?" Elicia said.

"Sorry. I need to get to the office. I've got a case file to review. Maybe later. Okay?"

Disappointment covered Elicia's features. But she shrugged in a good sport kind of gesture. Days later, she wasn't responding as kindly to his repeated refusals to resume healthy marital relations.

Brad knew his wife was getting fed up with his sudden lack of interest in sex, however, he was at a loss as to how he could overcome this newfound problem. He could not force himself to do what had always come so naturally. Every day that passed increased his sense of inner shame. With the shame came an outward expression of anger verging on rage. Yet, Brad would not tell his wife the truth of what he was dealing with. Weeks turned to months, while he isolated himself even more.

Five months after the life-altering auto erotica case, things reached an explosion point between Brad and Elicia. When she threatened divorce, he knew he had a choice. Either confess the crazy haunting thoughts that were destroying their marriage, or allow the tendrils of anxiety and depression over uninvited dreams, to steal the last vestige of his life.

Brad swallowed hard, and calmly asked his wife to sit down next to him. Without giving names, addresses, or other in appropriate information, he told her in graphic and honest detail, what was tormenting him. She immediately began to cry.

But as Elicia soon explained, her tears were from relief, because this was something they could work through. Brad felt like a thousand pound weight was lifted off his shoulders, as his own relief flooded in. His confession had triggered Elicia's mercy and support — and his hope.

Husband and wife teamed up to research. They landed on a psychologist whose website said he specialized in natural as well as scientific treatment for restoring a balanced sense of well-being. When he called, Brad took the first available appointment.

It shocked Brad to find it was much easier to tell a stranger his story than it had been to tell his wife. He was also surprised at how quickly the doctor was able to help him. For some unknown reason, the auto erotica case had prompted his mind to get stuck in a subconscious pattern of replay, but Brad's mind substituted his face for the victim who initiated it. But the doctor had answers.

After only a few sessions, the psychologist was able to help Brad break the annoying dream cycle and anxious thoughts, by using only natural methods. They discussed medications from the beginning, but Brad opted to wait and see if the other options worked first. Thankfully, they did.

The doctor taught Brad neuroplasticity techniques, focusing on relaxation through meditation and prayer, something Brad hadn't done since childhood. He was surprised to discover how easily he returned to conversations with God, and how comforting they were.

Brad's psychologist also started him on a healthier eating regimen, including a daily dose of pomegranate juice, ginseng, and vitamin D, all touted to help men with sexual dysfunction issues. His other prescriptions incorporated consistent sleep at night, a reduction in caffeine and increase in water, regular exercise, and Epsom Salt baths three to four nights a week, to improve his magnesium absorption.

Within thirty days, Brad felt nearly normal. He was sleeping deeper without disturbing dream disruptions, had more energy, and his sex life with his wife had resumed. By finally revealing his secret, he had set himself free.

## Profiling Brad's Reactions

Inevitably, if you work enough calls, you're going to see crazy displays of humanity, like Brad did on this auto erotica case. Sometimes, the images don't dissipate into memory obscurity, but instead begin to follow us, even disrupting our personal lives. Trying to ignore these issues does not ultimately work.

"With confession comes mercy," is a proverb well remembered in these situations. Often, our fear about someone else's reactions are worse than what reality proves true. We can't heal what we don't acknowledge.

## Questions to Consider

- **When should Brad have talked to his wife about what was bothering him?**
- **Are there steps Brad could have taken to protect his mind from emotional overload and maintain his objectivity in the face of a strange scene?**
- **What fears might Brad have faced when considering professional assistance?**

## C.O.D.E. Conduct

**Communication** — No matter what is weighing on your mind, remind yourself that it is not too late. Make this a mantra in your mind, so you can take positive steps toward a resolution, instead of allowing a past experience to paralyze your present.

**Objectiveness** — Look at the facts of your situation, and ask yourself what you would advise someone you cared about who was going through a similar struggle. Don't allow uncontrollable emotions to control your objective perspective.

**Dedication** — Dedicate yourself to honesty above all. You don't have to give your significant other all of the graphic details, but you do need to tell them enough so they understand why you are troubled. Prove your willingness to do whatever it takes to help your relationships to survive, and act on what will help it flourish.

**Engagement** — Don't hide from uncomfortable emotions by pushing the disconnect button and reacting in anger. If you do, ignoring your family can become a habit that jeopardizes your relationships, while pushing colleagues away could cost you a career.

## Chapter 4
## The Tightening Noose

Deputy Davis met Hunter Thomas at her car and escorted her to the garage on scene. A white male hung partially suspended from a ligature around his neck, made from a pulley drive belt and a bungee cord.

A paramedic with NCCAD walked alongside Hunter and said, "We checked for signs of life and the heart monitor shows no activity."

Thomas ran the strip and looked at her watch to pronounce. "Time of death, 17:47."

She then photographed the scene and did a cursory body exam for any other injuries. After that, she took the liver temp — after three minutes, the reading was 99.1 degrees with an ambient temperature of 36 degrees. Thomas found it odd that the man was dressed in several shirts, a hoodie, with a heavy outer coat.

After Hunter finished the scene exam and documented the facts, she released the corpse and placed it in a body bag to prepare the victim for transport. But before she left the scene, Hunter was cornered by a woman who identified herself as the man's step-daughter. She was not happy.

"Where are you taking my dad?"

Hunter breathed deep to ensure her response came across as gentle and compassionate, not always easy with a screamer in your face. "What's your name?"

"Veronica. Now answer my question. Where are you taking Dad?"

Hunter exhaled. "We'll take him back to the county morgue to get him ready for whatever kind of service you decide on."

"You're doing an autopsy, right?"

Hunter's mind whirled, as she considered how to respond to the woman's question. She envisioned the dingy, makeshift facility that served as their small county morgue. With few funds and fewer ancillary resources, her ability to perform any autopsies, except those of absolute necessity, was hindered. This case appeared to be an obvious suicide, so it did not fit the criteria to pull from the county's limited budget.

"Can you tell me about your dad's last few days?"

"What's that got to do with my question? You need to do an autopsy. He didn't leave a note. My dad would not do something like this without leaving a note."

Hunter noted that she did not say her dad would not commit suicide. *Family members often subconsciously know more than they are willing to accept in cases like this,* Hunter postulated to herself. "My question is actually part of the investigation. I'm trying to determine any unusual behavior that might tell us something about his mental state just prior to the event."

The woman's shoulders slumped slightly. "I hadn't seen him for about three hours, but that's not unusual. Dad likes to walk in the woods behind our house, and sometimes, he goes all the way to the back of our property to watch the neighbor's horses. He can disappear for an entire day when he does that, so I didn't think much about not seeing him for that length of time. But then the dog got out of the house and ran to the garage. I took off after her, and when I got inside the garage, I couldn't believe it."

"What has his mood been like recently?"

"That's why I don't think he killed himself. He's been depressed and angry for months. I'm not sure why. But the past couple of days, he cheered up. I hadn't seen him that happy for a really long time. I had my dad back. So you need to do an autopsy, because someone must have done this to him."

"Veronica, I understand how confusing all of this must be..."

She cut Hunter off. "Don't tell me you understand how I feel. This man did not have to take me in, but he did. I was a nine-year-old brat who only thought of herself, and then Craig came into my mom's life. From the start, he treated me like his own. And when Mom died a few years ago, he never abandoned me. He stood by me, comforted me, protected me, and he was nothing but fatherly. He is my rock."

Hunter instantly felt compassion for the woman. "I'm sorry. I did not mean to diminish your pain. I'll certainly do everything I can to find answers."

"I still want an autopsy."

"Expect to hear from me in a few days. When I have findings to report."

"After the autopsy?"

"After I've finished an extensive exam."

Hunter felt bad circumventing the truth with the young woman standing in front of her. But she knew the daughter neither wanted to hear, nor would she fully comprehend, the financial roadblock Hunter faced in trying to meet her request.

At the morgue, Hunter conducted a more extensive body exam and found no trauma or signs of abuse. She collected blood for toxicology, and sent the panels to the lab for processing. Everything came back negative.

Veronica was not satisfied when she called with the news. "What did the autopsy results show?"

"Remember, I told you..."

"And I told you to do an autopsy. My dad did not kill himself."

*Here we go,* Hunter thought.

She was right.

Veronica's voice escalated to a screech. "I demand an autopsy. You have to do it. It's your job."

"Ma'am, we just don't have the funds to do a nonessential autopsy. And in your step-father's case, there is no evidence to indicate the need to do one."

"And I'm telling you, my dad's autopsy *is* essential. Who are you to make that determination?"

Hunter braced herself before speaking. "I am your county coroner. It is my job to make these kinds of determinations."

"Then I'll go above your head. I'll make you do one. And I'll make your life miserable until it's finished."

She kept her word.

For weeks, Veronica badgered. At least once a day, she called the coroner's office, the county commissioners, the health department, she even called the governor's office. Hunter could hardly focus for all of the chaos the woman caused. She sympathized with Veronica's grief, but she was interfering with her work on other cases. It wasn't until a sheriff's deputy had to threaten harassment charges, that Veronica stopped. Mostly.

Nearly a year later however, Hunter caught a break that finally put the matter to rest.

When she heard Veronica on the phone, Hunter's instinct was to hang up — but that would not be professional. So she stifled a groan and said, "Hello, Veronica. How are you?"

"Embarrassed, actually."

Intrigued, Hunter stayed silent.

"I. Well. I found. I found a note from Dad."

Hunter sat up straighter in her chair. "You found a note?"

As soon as it came out of her mouth, he realized how redundant the question was.

Veronica spoke in a soft, slow tone. "I finally got around to cleaning out the garage. I kept putting it off, you know? Anyway, this morning, I went out to tackle it. One of the first things I did was to open up Dad's tool box. He was always tinkering with something. I should have known. But I didn't think. I'm so sorry, Ms. Thomas. The note was in there — in his tool box. Can I read it to you?"

All the months of frustration melted from Hunter's heart. "Of course."

Veronica paused before starting.

*My Precious Daughter,*

*God never blessed me with a birth child, but that's because he was saving his best for later, when he delivered you into my life. I thank God every day for you. Please forgive me for this, and understand it has nothing to do with my love for you. No father could ask for more than you've given me through the years. But I'm so tired and I miss your mom. I've lived a good life, and I'm ready for whatever comes next. Take care of yourself for me, sweet girl. I'll be looking out for you.*

*Forever Family,*
*Dad*

Veronica sniffled. Hunter's own eyes were wet.

"You were right all along," she said. "I really feel bad about all of my accusations."

Hunter felt no desire to right-fight. "Don't worry about it, I'm just happy you have some closure now."

47

"I finally feel at peace for the first time since all of this happened. Will you forgive me?"

"Consider it done," Hunter said.

"Thank you." The line clicked off.

One of Hunter's biggest headaches came in the form of financial constraints that sometimes felt like a tightening noose. But when a decedent's family wanted her to use resources that were neither reasonable or affordable, it made the job even more difficult. However, she was glad she had kept her cool with the woman. In death investigations, you never knew how things would ultimately turn out. In this case, peace was possible because professionalism had prevailed.

## Profiling Hunter's Reactions

Tight finances is one of the greatest challenges any agency must contend with — especially when you are operating in a small community with a tiny budget. Add familial emotions into the stress recipe already stirred with a traumatic event, few operating funds, and questionable facts, and the heat can rise quickly.

Hunter's ability to respond professionally under personal attack, meant the door was open when new evidence became available. It is never easy to remain cool, calm, and collected when unfair accusations are thrown your way, but no one wins in a fight to be right. We don't know what tomorrow holds, so it's important to imagine ourselves in the shoes of the person we are in conflict with — this way the door is always open to a peaceful result. Remember to always be the most reasonable person in the room.

## Questions to Consider

- **How could Hunter have dealt with the grieving daughter better?**
- **What impact did Hunter's financial constraints have on her job performance in this case?**
- **If Hunter had allowed her emotions to dictate her actions, how might this situation have turned out differently?**

## C.O.D.E. Conduct

**Communication** — Even when you feel badgered by someone demanding answers you can't give, communicate what you can as often as you can. The unknown is one of the most frightening and anger-inducing things a victim's family will face.

**Objectiveness** — Guard yourself against assumptions or preconceived opinions about people or what evidence appears to suggest. Many times, the future brings surprising revelations, but an open mind is required to see what the facts shed light on.

**Dedication** — No matter how you are treated, commit to remaining true to the values, policies, integrity, and professionalism your position requires. You cannot be truly effective if you do not possess these crucial qualities.

**Engagement** — The temptation to ignore, withdraw, or react negatively is strong when you are being pressured. But with every interaction, treat each person you serve as if this was the first time you saw them and their concerns were the most important elements in the biggest case of your life. Offering respect and dignity to all human beings is a way to make a real difference in the world and on your job.

## 9-1-1 Dispatcher Summary

9-1-1. Three numbers that could determine life or death for the American public. In the U.K., the numbers are 9-9-9. In New Zealand, they are 1-1-2. In Australia, 0-0-0 connects a desperate dialer with a voice that can get them help. But no matter what country a person is in, the critical importance of emergency switchboard operators is the same — without them, many more people across the globe would die.

Dispatchers are often forced to listen helplessly to some of the most gruesome situations any person can endure, yet civilians likely don't think about the human beings on the other end of their desperate lifeline. Nor, do they consider the impact of long-term exposure to volatile emotions and unusual drama. Dispatchers often develop a dark sense of humor, as a way to cope.

Typically, the training for emergency dispatchers is minimal, the pay is low, considering the responsibilities of the job, with modest raises at best. Some operators work swing shifts which are hard on the body, mind, and the spirit, and forced overtime happens far too often, when there's a shortage of people to work. All of these factors can create mental distractions, triggered by financial worries, fatigue, and frustration. To complicate things further, dispatch centers can't always afford the education and certifications needed for their dispatchers. But that one caller who says thank you, that one case where a life is saved, that one shift where everything goes right, makes serving worthwhile.

This section is dedicated to those driven to help the callers who light up their lines, despite all of these obstacles. May you know that every ounce of angst, fatigue, and personal sacrifice are deeply appreciated. Thank you!

## Chapter 5
## Texting Tragedy

Josie answered the familiar notes of an incoming call. "9-1-1. What is your emergency?"

"Accident. I need help. There's been an accident."

"Okay sir, stay calm. Are you hurt? Were you in the accident?"

"No ma'am. I just drove up on it. Looks like it just happened. Single car. It looks like it drove right off the highway and plowed into a tree. I don't see skid marks or anything."

Josie typed as the man provided details, dispatching fire, ambulance, and law enforcement. "Can you tell if anyone is in the vehicle, sir?"

The man huffed as he spoke, indicating movement. "I'm walking up to it now."

"What's your location, sir?"

"I'm on Highway 49, about four miles out of Maddox."

Josie didn't have to pull up the map. Maddox was her own hometown suburb, small enough where almost everybody knew everybody, and the headquarters for their county's 9-1-1 dispatch office. This caller was about four miles from where Josie sat right then. Her heart sped up.

Suddenly, the caller half gasped and half cried. "Oh no. O God. How awful."

"Sir? What's happening, sir?" Josie spoke silently to herself. *Please don't let it be any of my family or close friends.*

The man spoke through tears, "It's a girl. She looks young."

A single, loud sob heaved across the phone line. Then,

under weighted breaths he continued, "She's torn up. Bad. Oh man. I think she might be dead. She's not moving and there's blood everywhere. She has blonde hair, but right now, most of it's dripping with red."

For a split moment, Josie's imagination tried to take over her mind. *Is it someone I know? My niece, Stephie just got her license and she's a blonde.*

Josie took an intentional deep breath and admonished herself. *Stop. Get a grip. Stay focused on the job.* "Okay sir, I know this is difficult, but I need you to hold it together. Help is on the way."

"Tell them to hurry. Except I'm afraid it's too late for her."

Josie forced herself to maintain a professional composure, though adrenalin flooded her veins and her blood pressure pumped more powerfully than it did during most calls. Something about this one felt different. And it was more than location, something in Josie's gut told her she wasn't going to like the outcome. She would soon find out her gut was absolutely right.

The caller hung up after the first responders arrived on scene, but the tension in the air of the 9-1-1 office did not dissipate. Across squawking radios, it was evident in all of the voices attending the accident; county deputies, state highway patrol, and EMS, something wasn't being said. There was a vibe that said there was something uniquely wrong. Moments like this made the physical disconnect between 9-1-1 and those who worked directly with victims feel like a punch in the stomach. Josie wished she could know exactly what was going on.

It would take over an hour before she found out why everyone seemed exceptionally on edge. Sergeant Troy Matthews walked into the office, his face so low it appeared as if his chin might drag the ground.

Sergeant Matthews made his way directly to Josie. "You took the call about the girl out on 49?"

Tears pooled in Josie's eyes. "Yes."

Troy, whose own eyes glistened, placed his hand on Josie's shoulder."It was Mandy Sellers' daughter, Bella."

Josie raised out of her chair instinctively, "What? No. Not Bella! She—we— all of us loved. . . ."

"I know," Troy broke in. "It was like she belonged to all of us, like she was our own daughter."

Josie fell back onto the seat, Mandy was a well-respected sheriff's deputy who had been on the force for over fifteen years. "I—we. We practically raised her with Mandy. After she started school, she came every day when they let out. In the summer, she ran and got us lunch, or on really hot days, a small vanilla cone for both of us. From the time she was a little thing, she had been a bright light and energizing force that lifted our spirits on mundane or difficult days. We all looked forward to her visits, I can't imagine her not bouncing through the door."

Troy nodded his head in agreement. "I know what you mean. Her innocence made you remember the good in this world — something it's easy to forget in this line of work."

The 9-1-1 line lit up requiring Josie's immediate attention. In that instant, Josie knew the expectation. Turn your feelings off and turn the calm on. She had no choice but to delay her grief until later.

But one thought disturbed Josie the most as she turned to take the call. *How did Bella die?*

Josie shoveled her emotions deep into the recesses of her soul and pushed past her thoughts to make it through the rest of her shift. It was when she climbed into her car that everything bubbled up and washed over her. Right before leaving, Josie's supervisor told her how the accident had happened. Bella's eyes must have left the road — she likely veered off while typing the unfinished text they found on her phone.

Josie clutched the steering wheel, unable to make her hand turn the ignition to start her car. Her sobs ricocheted off the interior windows and dashboard, her own cries pelting her ears.

After several minutes, Josie transitioned to hiccups. She shouted through them at the roof. "Why Bella? Honey, we talked about texting and driving so many times. I know your mom had those conversations with you too. You promised." Josie dropped her chin toward her chest and whispered, "You promised."

A somber cloud hung over the community in the weeks following Bella's death. But for Josie and her 9-1-1 teammates, as well as local ambulance and fire crews, plus city, county, and many state law enforcement officers, the gray cloud refused to blow away so quickly.

Though everyone struggled to screw on a mask of normalcy, no one could bear its heavy weight for long periods of time. When one slipped, sadness, anger, or denial would spill from the person, causing an awkwardness to fill the room — yet few would talk about it. Instead, everyone ducked their heads and tried to pretend the slip never occurred. Mostly, no one mentioned Bella's name.

Sometimes, Josie pondered why they all avoided talking about the beautiful young ray of light was extinguished too soon. She guessed that everyone wrestled with the same confusing emotions she did.

Many days, Josie denied her anger at Bella for doing one of the most dangerous things she was warned against. Sadness crept in when Josie imagined all of the things Bella might have done with her life if she'd lived. But the most painful occurred when Josie forgot Bella was gone, glanced at the clock, and momentarily thought she would breeze in the door just to say hi.

Josie always adapted and resolved to make it through her shift, but there were a handful of instances when she had to take a bathroom break, so she could have another solid cry. She often longed to talk to someone, but few seemed willing and no professional help was offered. Josie coped the only way she knew how. She swallowed her grief, hoping it would eventually go away — and in some form it did. Temporarily.

Eight years later, after the umpteenth time of driving past Bella's crash site, triggered by vivid imaginings of those horrific final moments, Josie finally woke up. She realized there was a pattern to her bouts of insomnia, nightmares, anxiety attacks, and erratic eating. She needed professional help.

Josie gave herself permission to seek out a grief counselor, and began weekly sessions. Ready to heal, she made rapid progress, and the counselor soon shifted Josie to monthly visits. Within six months, she felt like a new person and felt she had processed the unresolved grief she'd tried to avoid for so long.

The sun hung low on a warm summer evening when Josie sat at the foot of Bella's grave. She held two small vanilla cones in her hands, symbols of a special bond and a sign of Josie's forgiveness. After finally asking for help, Josie was able to let go.

### Profiling Josie's Reactions

The fact that Josie's painful memories surfaced weeks, months, or years after experiencing a loss or traumatic event, is actually normal. If you think of people as being like volcanoes, and human feelings like magma, you can see how pushing emotional pain down builds pressure that at some point, must escape.

If you don't intentionally find healthy vents to release steams of anger, sadness, frustration, grief, etc., at some point, you can expect an emotional explosion. Sadly, these eruptions often happen at an inopportune time. Intentionality is the key to protecting yourself and others from the damage of painful experiences on the job.

### Questions to Consider

- **What symptoms did Josie have that mirror Post Traumatic Stress Disorder?**
- **How might Josie and her colleagues have supported each other and strengthened their departmental work in the process?**
- **Where could Josie have turned to work through her grief sooner?**

### C.O.D.E. Conduct

**Communication** — Many counselors say grief is what you feel inside, and mourning is the outward expression of grief. In order to truly heal from loss or trauma, you must both grieve and mourn. Share your emotions by talking with a safe person you can trust.

**Objectiveness** — If you find you are often emotionally triggered by environment, scent, sounds, or other connections to past events, allow yourself to face and deal with the origin of that pain. Are you struggling to sleep at night? Eating poorly? Lethargic? Anxious? Try to view yourself as an outsider might, or pretend these things are happening to someone close to you. What kind of advice would you give them? Now take it yourself.

**Dedication** — Memorializing a loss through volunteerism or founding a social cause can provide a sense of purpose born from the pain. Dedicating time and energy for the benefit of others takes nothing away from the person(s) who are gone, but can honor them and keep their memory alive indefinitely.

**Engagement** — Participate in conversations and activities that honor the dead. Don't run from reminders or avoid sharing grief. Openness helps us heal faster and more deeply. Don't let a loss stop you from connecting to other people. We all need someone. If you feel like you don't, that's a waving red flag pointing to the likelihood of a past that's holding you hostage.

# Chapter 6
# Mother Murder

Richelle, or Rikki as family and friends called her, settled into her chair for her 9-1-1 operator shift. The morning had started unusually well. Rikki was able to get the kids up, fed, dressed, and ready for school without a fight, something that rarely happened with her early schedule. Leaving home, she turned back toward the door, taking in a final glimpse of her three children who weren't babies any more.

Thirteen-year-old Dillon smiled widely, shook his mocha colored bangs out of his golden brown eyes and said, "Bye Mom. See ya later."

"Make sure you and your brother and sister don't miss the bus."

With a light and playful tone to his voice, Dillon said, "I always do."

As Rikki closed the door, she thought to herself, *I am blessed with three of the greatest kids on the planet. I need to remember to tell them how much I appreciate them. I should do something nice with them when I get paid.*

But as she backed out of her driveway, Rikki's thoughts had already drifted from home to work. Her occupation required laser-sharp focus and she had to mentally prepare long before her shift officially started. One minor distraction could cost a human life, and as a single mother, she could not afford to lose her job.

The moment Rikki took her seat in the office, the line lit up. "9-1-1, what is your emergency," she said in her practiced, professional tone.

There was no emotion in the female voice that responded.

She sounded flat, deadpan, disconnected, robotic —even matter-of-fact. "I need an ambulance at my house."

"What's your address?"

"410 Moss Road."

"What's your name?"

The caller mumbled, "Brenda Lincoln."

"Lincoln?"

"Yeah."

"What's your emergency?"

"I shot my kids and I cut my wrists."

"Did you say you shot your kids?"

"Yeah."

"How do you spell your last name?"

"L.I.N.C.O.L.N."

"Where are the children now?"

"In my daughter's room."

"In your daughter's room?"

"Yeah."

"Where are you?"

"In the living room. My husband wants a divorce. He said he's going to take my kids from me. I can't let him take my babies."

"How old are your children?"

"Seven and three."

Rikki typed her notes fiercely. "Okay. And...you said you cut your wrists? Are you bleeding?"

"Yeah. There's blood everywhere."

"And where is the gun and knife you used?"

"In my living room."

"Are you still armed?"

"No. It's in my children's room."

Something didn't make sense to Rikki. "Brenda, you said the gun and knife were in the living room, but you just said it's in your children's room. Can you clarify for me? Where exactly is the gun, and where is the knife?"

"The knife is with me in the living room. I think I dropped the gun in Chelsea's room. She was the last one I shot. But I'm really not sure now."

Rikki couldn't get used to the lack of emotion some people displayed when they communicated emergencies, but this was the worst she'd ever experienced. By far. "Where's your husband right now?"

"Downstairs."

"Do you have a split-level home, or is downstairs a basement?"

"Yeah. Basement."

"What's your husband's condition?"

"I don't know. I haven't talked to him."

"Okay. What's his name?"

"Canaan."

"Canaan Lincoln?"

"Yeah."

"And do you have any other weapons with you?"

"No."

"What are you feeling right now?"

"I'm tired. I took a lot of Benadryl."

At least that explained some of the woman's emotional disconnect — that and the serious shock the woman was likely in. "Is the front door unlocked?"

"Yeah."

"Is there anyone else in the residence besides you, your children, and your husband."

"My mom's on the way. I gotta go. I'm tired."

"Brenda, don't hang up. Stay on the line. I need you to keep talking to me. Emergency responders are on the way. Can you assure me you're not going to try and hurt any of them?"

"I won't. I'm laying down on the couch. Hey, my mom's here now. You want to talk to her?"

"Yes."

A more mature sounding woman got on the phone. "Hello."

"What's your name, ma'am?"

"Renee." Oh my God. My grandbabies.

"Have you found the children?"

Amidst deep sobs, "No. No. But my daughter told me she killed them." Hysteria found its way into the older woman's voice.

"Ma'am, ma'am, I need you to calm down. Your daughter said the children are in the bedroom on the floor. Can you locate them for me?"

The woman's sobs grew in intensity to the point she was incoherent, her breathing stilted and broken. Rikki heard the woman lay the phone down and walk away, her cries reverberating through the phone line as if she were still holding it to her mouth. Suddenly, a blood clotting scream caused Rikki's heart to nearly stop in her chest, followed by a guttural cry, "Oh my God, no! Brenda, what have you done?"

It was obvious Renee had found her grandchildren.

A man's agonized echoes began to scream in harmony with the traumatized grandmother's. Apparently, the husband had heard the commotion and made his way upstairs. Sirens played in the background, and Rikki's screen alerted her to the simultaneous arrival of law enforcement, EMS, and fire. The last thing Rikki heard before the line went silent was the father shouting, "My God, my God, how am I supposed to live without my kids?"

Goosebumps purpled Rikki's arms as she briefly allowed herself to imagine how the family might feel. Those kinds of thoughts attacked her mind off and on throughout the day — no matter how she tried, she could not push them completely away. The office clock seemed to tick in slow motion.

Somehow, Rikki kept it together while she was on shift, but when she was completely alone in the parking lot of the dispatch office, her response to the tragedy physically took her to her knees. She kept asking herself, *How could a mother do this to her own flesh?* In that instant, life with her children took on new meaning. Rikki's earlier thought about focusing more on her kids became a solid commitment to herself.

When Rikki arrived home, she clutched Dillon and her two younger children so tight that all three squirmed to escape her hug.

Dillon complained, "Gosh, what's the deal?"

Rikki had already screwed her brave face tightly in place before she walked in. "I just love you guys...that's all."

"We know. All right."

Rikki faked a laugh, "Can't a mom show her kids how much they mean to her without being given a hard time for it?"

"We love you too, Mom. But sometimes you're weird."

Rikki laughed and tussled Dillon's hair. She'd take weird.

It took several months and consistent guidance from a counselor for Rikki to stop having nightmares over the mother murder call. But over time, and by facing the impact of its shadowy imprint on her soul, she was able to process her emotions in a healthy way. But she also learned a life-changing lesson. Rikki never took her children for granted in the same way again — and she developed a fresh appreciation for how she and her ex-husband were able to set aside their differences to keep the focus on the innocents they brought into the world.

## Profiling Rikki's Reactions

9-1-1 dispatchers hear some of the worst and most shocking extremes of human nature. Like most, Rikki was able to set her personal life aside while on the job, until a call came in that hit too close to her personal life. When she took the disturbing mother-murder call; it pushed a sensitive soul button inside Rikki. But she showed wisdom by seeking counseling early.

Rikki gave herself permission to face and walk through the steps of grief, realizing that though the children were faceless to her, she still mourned their loss. Ultimately, through professional guidance, she was able to use the experience to remind her not to take her children for granted.

## Questions to Consider

- **Was there anything Rikki could have done in advance to prepare herself for this type of call?**
- **What might have happened to Rikki had she not sought professional help?**
- **How could Rikki turn this tragic call into the catalyst for a greater purpose?**

## C.O.D.E. Conduct

**Communication** — People instinctually try to run from their emotions and ignore bad memories, choosing not to talk about the painful situation and shutting down if others try to bring the subject up. However, mental health experts repeatedly state that talking with an appropriate person about our pain can help us heal.

**Objectiveness** — Don't beat yourself up for grieving over unseen or unnamed victims you are exposed to. It's normal to feel sorrow at any loss, especially when children are victimized. You can and should expect to deal with PTSD at some point in your career. If it doesn't happen, great, you fall into an uncommon statistical category. But if you do experience post-traumatic stress, remember that PTSD is a normal reaction to abnormal stress. And you are often exposed to situations the general public never knows exist.

**Dedication** — Especially when traumatized, commit yourself to self-care. An empty cup has nothing to pour into others. Protect yourself, so you are equipped to serve others.

**Engagement** — It's smart to participate in therapy after a traumatic event. There's nothing wrong with seeking help — in reality, it makes you wise, strong, and insightful. Give yourself permission to engage with a professional if needed. See our resource list at the end of the book.

# Chapter 7
# School Zone

Ben flipped two large, round pancakes onto Shawn's plate, covering its porcelain surface. *How did time pass so quickly?*

Ben's mind replayed a scene from eight years earlier when he had scooped two much smaller flapjacks onto Shawn's airplane shaped plate. Back then, his six-year-old son had bounced in his chair shouting, "Thank you, Daddy. My tummy's hungry." Ben still remembered how his son's innocent words had made him laugh.

Now, Ben barely got a grunt from his fourteen-year-old. *So much for gratitude.*

In front of the school, Shawn practically leaped from the car to escape Ben's presence.

"Have a good. . . ." Shawn slammed the door before Ben could finish his sentence.

"Single parenting stinks," Ben said to the empty seat beside him. Then he shrugged as he pulled away, not knowing that only two hours later he would desperately wish he could have a re-do of this moment.

At the office, Ben poured steaming coffee into his stainless steel thermal cup before sitting down at his assigned work station. These days, there was little time for small talk between 9-1-1 operators — it seemed the lines never stopped lighting up.

The morning was fairly routine for their Southern Cal community. Ben's calls included a reported home invasion, a woman in labor at a busy shopping plaza, two drug overdoses, and three traffic accidents. All were part of a normal day on the job, though one did require an on-scene extraction. But the call that came in at 10:08 a.m. changed the day. . .and Ben's life.

Ben had just returned from the restroom and a coffee refill, when he logged back into his computer at 10:06 a.m. The lines were oddly quiet.

Stephanie, who sat a few feet away, teased, "You know it's not a good sign when the lines aren't lighting."

Ben frowned. "Don't jinx us."

A low, throaty chuckle was the only response Stephanie had time to make. Simultaneously, all of their boards lit up at once. There were more calls than operators to field them. Nothing could have prepared Ben for what the voice on the other end of the line was going to say.

"9-1-1, what is your emergency?" Ben said in his professional voice.

In a hushed tone, a woman cried. "Help. We need help." It sounded like fireworks were going off in the background. Ben knew that sound though — they were definitely not fireworks.

"Ma'am, what is your emergency?" Ben could hear the forced calm in his co-workers, all having similar conversations with their callers, from what he could hear of their sides of their dialogues.

Ben's pulled his attention back to his caller.

"He's shooting us. Please don't let him find me. Please send someone to help us. We need help now. I don't want to die."

Ben straightened in his chair. "Ma'am, I understand you're scared, and I'm going to get you help. But I need you to tell me your name and where you are."

"My name is Mary Villa. I'm hiding in the library. In the closet. Please hurry. Please."

A prickly sensation started at the base of Ben's skull and traveled the entirety of his spine in mili-seconds. "Mary, which library are you at?"

"McArthur High. I'm the guidance counselor."

For a singular moment, Ben froze. His fingers stopped moving on the keyboard, and he forgot to breathe. Shawn attended McArthur High. Ben felt like his body disconnected, as if he were part of a hazy dream — surely a shooter was not lashing out in deadly rage at his son's school.

But in fact, it was no dream.

Stephanie hissed his name. "Ben. Ben. The best way for us to help Shawn right now is to do our jobs. Keep it together — for Shawn."

Ben nodded. Stephanie was already talking into her mouthpiece again.

"Okay Mary, tell me, are you alone?" While he listened to her answer, he typed out his dispatch for all available emergency personnel.

The terrified woman said, "No, I have three students in here with me."

Ben fought off his instinct to ask if Shawn was one of them. "Good. Now tell me, do you know the proximity of the shooter to your location?"

"Not exactly. I saw him walking down the hall with the guns in his hands."

"So he has more than one gun?"

"Yes, I saw two of them. And it looked like he had a lot of bullets. I saw him kick the door into Mr. Kendrick's room right before I ducked into the library. I gathered the only kids I saw, and we've been hiding in this closet ever since. I'm so scared he'll find us."

"Mary, I'm going to stay right here with you until you're safe. So you stay with me. Okay?"

"Okay." The woman's breathing slowed audibly, and she sounded less panicked.

Following protocol to help calm their callers, Ben asked a series of questions. "How long have you worked at McArthur, Mary?"

"This is my first year."

Ben remembered Shawn complaining about the new counselor. But in his current stage of life, Shawn complained about most adults. Ben only hoped he would get the chance to grow out of it.

"Have you always wanted to be a counselor?"

"No, but my high school guidance counselor really helped me. So, I decided I wanted to make a difference for kids like he did." Mary's voice almost sounded normal now, the distraction was working.

"Tell me about the kids who are with you. Are they boys? Girls?" Ben held his breath while he waited for the answer.

"I've got three of the junior boys."

*Shawn's a junior.* "What are their nam…"

From the phone line, a loud thud and a harmony of female and male screams interrupted the question Ben most wanted an answer to.

"Mary? Mary, tell me what's going on."

The sound of multiple shots answered Ben's probing. But he kept trying, not realizing that he was shouting. Shawn could have been with her. "Mary! Mary, tell me what's happening right now! Mary, are you okay?"

A crunching sound followed by the humming of a dead line were the only answers he got.

The weight of Ben's head became more than his neck could sustain. He propped his elbows on his desk, and let his face drop into his hands. Then Ben felt warmth on his shoulder.

"It's okay. Take a break, Ben," Becky, his supervisor said from directly behind him. He hadn't noticed she had stepped into his space.

"I can't," he said without turning around. "I'll take another line."

"We've got this. Just step away and catch your breath. You're too close to the situation."

"I'm fine, Becky. Really. There are more calls coming in than you can handle right now."

"True, but handle it we will. Without you."

Ben turned and faced his supervisor. "Please, I'm begging you. I need to keep my mind busy, or I'll go crazy. Either that, or I'm going to McArthur."

"You're not going anywhere." Becky sighed, "You can keep your composure?"

"Have I ever lost it on the job?"

"No. But you've never been in this kind of situation either."

Ben stood up. "Look, I'm scared out of my mind right now. Actually, I'm terrified that my son is already gone, and I don't know it. But if there's a chance that he's still alive, and I have to believe there is, then I need to do what I can do to help save him and the others trapped in that building."

"All right, you win. But I'm going to stay here with you." Becky had taken on a no-nonsense stance.

"Got it," Ben said as he turned around to take another call.

For three and a half more hours, Ben made himself focus on his work, while he silently prayed that Shawn was alive. But the screams of Mary and the male students with her haunted Ben's thoughts any time there was more than a second's pause. All awareness of bodily functions disappeared in that time. Ben felt no hunger or thirst, as adrenalin propelled him on.

During those additional hours, Ben coached several students and school staff with ways to protect themselves, until they were able to reach a place of safety. Thankfully, in talks with subsequent victims, he didn't hear bursts of bullets like those that ended his earlier call with Mary.

Suddenly, Ben heard Shawn's voice. But it wasn't on the phone line, it came from behind Ben, in the 9-1-1 office.

Becky booted Ben out of his seat and took over his call.

Ben could barely stand. His legs felt like pudding. He wanted to run to Shawn, but his body wouldn't obey his brain.

Shawn covered the distance for both of them. He ran to Ben and fell in his arms. Father and son clutched each other and cried openly. Neither thought or cared about onlookers. Besides, the people in the room were like family anyway.

"Dad! Dad!" Tears poured off of Shawn's face, and he wiped them away by nuzzling against Ben's chest.

Several minutes later, they reluctantly pulled apart, then sheepishly looked around. There was evidence that everyone was impacted by Shawn's survival. Every operator wore tears and red faces, while they worked with trembling fingers, but not one person stopped doing their job. Serving others always came first.

Ben looked down at Shawn. "How did you get out?" He stroked his son's cinnamon-tinted hair.

"Mrs. Ragsdale snuck me and a bunch of other kids out an emergency exit by the gym." Shawn looked Ben deeply in the eyes. "She didn't follow us though. She went back inside. The cops moved right in and pulled us away, so I don't know if she got out or not. I'm scared she didn't make it."

"I know, Buddy. But we can't worry about something we don't know yet. We'll keep checking," Ben assured his son.

Less than an hour later, the rampage ended when the shooter killed himself — but not before taking eleven lives. Nine students, one teacher, and the high school principal all died at the hands of a troubled young man. Mrs. Ragsdale was the heroic teacher who sacrificed her life to save others.

Shawn developed night terrors that started the first time he fell asleep, and they continued most nights after. Ben rocked his teenage son as if he were a toddler, brushing his hair and shushing his fears. This was not the catalyst Ben expected for renewing their bond, however, he would not miss the opportunity to show his child the support he needed.

Ben tried to work the day after the shooting, though Becky urged him to stay home. However, his attempt was futile. In less than thirty minutes, he knew he needed time off, so he took a medical sabbatical to care for himself and his son. Ben was wise enough to know that until he healed, he wasn't capable of taking care of others.

Ben and Shawn also joined a community support group for survivors, victim families, and those directly affected by the tragedy at McArthur High. Just knowing the mountains and valleys of emotions they were feeling were not crazy or unusual, helped them heal. It also gave Ben an extra dose of compassion for the people who called into 9-1-1 when he returned to the job sixty days later. He still had to maintain his composure and professionalism with a certain level of emotional distance, but he now understood it was possible to do so while feeling deeper empathy for the person on the other end of the line.

In less than a year's time, a new purpose presented itself to Ben and Shawn. They were asked to speak at a school in an adjoining county — Shawn from a student's perspective, and Ben from his role as a 9-1-1 operator. That purpose deepened the recovery for both son and father dramatically.

Ben would never forget what happened that day, but neither would he stop trying to prevent someone else from enduring a similar situation. If there was a chance that only one person could be saved from something he said in a speaking presentation, or while he was on the phone with them during a 9-1-1 call, his time and energy were well spent. He never wanted another parent to feel what he had felt on that dreadful day.

### Profiling Ben's Reactions

It happens rarely, but sometimes, a 9-1-1 call gets personal. In this case, Ben was able to maintain his professional composure for the greater good, but there would have been nothing wrong with him, had he needed to step away due to overwhelming emotions. Ultimately, Ben was also wise enough to give himself permission to take time off when necessary.

Don't expect more from yourself than you are capable of. You will hear this more than once as you read this book — the information is that important — treat yourself with the same professional courtesy and/or personal care you would show someone you respected or who mattered to you.

### Questions to Consider

- **How would you feel if you went through what Ben did on this terrible day?**
- **Should Ben have stepped away from taking calls due to his personal interests in the situation?**
- **What ways can emergency services personnel prepare themselves and their communities to deal with this kind of tragedy?**

# C.O.D.E. Conduct

**Communication** — Talk with people who can relate and truly understand what you have experienced. Sharing emotions with people who get it, can speed up the healing process for you and them.

**Objectiveness** — Doing your job does not require robotic disconnectedness. You can feel empathy for others while still doing your job professionally and effectively.

**Dedication** — Help others in memory of those who died. Take up a cause or start a new one that invests in the living, as a way to honor the dying. Don't allow survivor's guilt or "why" questions to eat you up. Use your emotional energy to support those who are dealing with fresh grief or sorrow.

**Engagement** — Make time and take time for self-care and relational tending. Allow what you've been through to strengthen bonds and deepen appreciation for your relationships.

# Chapter 8
# Smothered Calls

"9-1-1, what is your emergency?" Carrie said.

A woman answered. "I want to report a crime. There's a man driving down I-5 with his dog hanging out of the driver's side window. I'm following him right now."

Carrie Maddock felt confused. "Did you say he committed a crime?"

"Yes, ma'am."

"Can you tell me if the driver is wearing a seat belt?"

After a brief pause, the woman answered. "Yes, he is."

Carrie typed the details in a side stream to law enforcement dispatch. "Is he texting while he's driving?"

"No ma'am. Both of his hands are on the steering wheel."

"Is he driving above the speed limit?"

The woman sighed. "No, but his dog has its head stuck out of the window. You need to have the police pull him over, he's breaking the law. It's animal endangerment."

Carrie's screen lit with an incoming message from the dispatcher she was communicating with. *Tell the caller that letting your dog get some fresh air is not breaking a law.*

Carrie relayed the message.

The woman was not happy. "What do you mean it's not illegal? It has to be. You don't know what you're talking about." Then the woman disconnected the call.

Within seconds, she called 9-1-1 again, re-explaining her concerns. She told Carrie's co-worker, "The previous operator apparently didn't know the law. I need someone to stop this man before he kills someone. Now!"

The woman's unhappiness grew when a supervisor had to tell her, "If you don't stop calling 9-1-1 on this matter, you could be charged for abuse of emergency communications."

The woman hung up in a huff, while Carrie got a chuckle. It turned out to be a night of humor.

An hour later, another caller struck Carrie's funny bone. A young man who sounded like he was between twenty and thirty answered Carrie's question regarding the reason for his emergency with heavy breathiness. "Something's wrong."

"What's the problem, sir?"

"I can't get it open. I've tried everything. What can I do?"

"What are you trying to get open?" Carrie said.

"The trunk on my car. It won't open with my key fob, and I have no idea how to get into it now."

Carrie thought what she didn't dare say, *Are you kidding me?*

Instead, she maintained professional protocol. "Does your car have a lock on the trunk?"

"Yeah."

"One with a key hole?"

"Yeah."

"Did you try to use the key to unlock the trunk?"

The man paused, and Carrie could hear a scratching sound in the background. Then he spoke. "Wow, it worked. Now, why didn't I think of that?"

Carrie shook her head at the computer screen. *Some people just don't use their brains.*

It was one of those days.

A sixteen-year-old girl called in from her gym class at the local high school. She was in a panic and could hardly get the words out. Finally, she blurted out what was causing her so much anxiety. "There's a squirrel on top of a telephone pole at the school, and it's not coming down. I think it's stuck. You need to send help right away."

Carrie had to stifle a laugh. But before getting off the line to take the next call, she assured the young lady that the squirrel was simply enjoying the beautiful day and would come down when it was ready.

*All in a day's work.*

Carrie's last call on her shift was an all too familiar one though. She never got used to hearing sad victims. She had a soft place in her heart for the elderly people who called to say, "I'm so lonely. Could you just talk to me?"

Carrie always felt guilty having to rush them off the phone. Any one of them could have been her own grandparent.

A few days later, after one of the biggest natural disasters their area had ever seen, Carrie's mind went to the many lonely callers she'd spoken to over the years. They made her think of her favorite uncle, who took his own life after her aunt left him.

When the hurricane finally dissipated, most thought the worst was over. But an oppressive heat wave rode its coattails. Smothering humidity, growing mold, airborne bacterium, waterborne illnesses, lack of water or food, and no electricity, put lives in jeopardy. The soupy days following created a thick mix of almost unbreathable conditions, and residents had no way to cool things down.

For people like Carrie, the worst part was that the storm had kept 9-1-1 operators in their homes, unable to do their jobs when they were needed the most. But the high waters spurred by the historic hurricane receded as fast as the rivers and tributaries rose, finally allowing Carrie and her co-workers to get back to the office. Now the problem was the rising tide of 9-1-1 calls.

Many people were in trouble, especially the elderly. Yet there was one group of people Carrie and her co-workers did not hear from — the residents of the Spring Hill Care Center.

After her first long week back, Carrie was watching TV when the news broke. She could not believe what the reporter was saying. This could not be happening — not in her town. Not to the people in her community. Not to those she spent the majority of her waking hours striving to serve, especially those who were the most fragile.

The newscaster's comments made Carrie feel sick.

"Early reports tell us that six people are dead and at least thirteen more are seriously ill, after the hurricane ripped a roof off a local convenience store and slung it into an electric transformer, knocking out power to the air conditioning system of Spring Hill Care Center. Residents baked in the sweltering heat, while employees were instructed to use fans, but not to call for outside help when people started getting sick."

Confusion reeled through Carrie's mind. *I could have helped those people if only someone would have called. Why wouldn't they alert us? Did they try when we couldn't get to the office? Why didn't they call until we answered?*

The reporter continued, "So far, the owners and managers of the facility have offered no explanation or defense for the deaths of the residents in their care. Instead of calling 9-1-1, calls were made to the mayor's office, leaving many perplexed. No names have been released at this time, however, we have been told that one of the victims was a ninety-one-year-old woman."

Carrie bit her nails, imagining the agony and suffering that poor little lady endured as her body began to shut down. *What were her last thoughts? Did she have children? Grandchildren? Great grandchildren?*

Carrie thought of her own grandmother. *How would I feel if Grandma Dalia was left to suffocate in a facility, smothered from the heat? If I was at my desk, could I have helped save the woman who died?*

That first report spurred a compulsive binge-watching habit for Carrie. She could not get enough of the reports about the nursing home tragedy. She watched at home, on breaks at work, at lunch, and over dinner. Consciously and subconsciously, the story affected Carrie. In a matter of days, it had even disrupted her sleep patterns as she woke up periodically to check for news updates. Being single meant there was no one to question her unhealthy new routine. She was careful not to let it affect her on the job, but any moment she was off, Carrie's obsessive following of the situation worsened. She couldn't let it go. But why?

One evening after work. Carrie was scrolling through her favorite news app when a breaking news notification popped up. Another tragedy had just come to light. Carrie laid her phone down and picked up the remote, flipping on the TV. An account of the new situation was airing.

A young, blonde reporter maintained a rigid stance and grim face as she spoke. "Another group of vulnerable people were denied rescue on the heels of the hurricane that devastated our city. Sources have revealed a home for the mentally challenged had hindered their employees from calling 9-1-1. The defenseless inhabitants of Skilled Horizons desperately needed help when the cooling unit servicing their building was damaged from wind-blown debris."

The reporter continued. "At this time, we have confirmed that at least two people are dead, a twenty-three-year-old male and a twenty-four-year-old female, with an undisclosed number of residents evacuated to area hospitals. This, after nine elderly people died from heat-related problems in the Spring Hill Care Center — only five blocks away. The police department told us that an ongoing criminal investigation into the agencies is underway. Both businesses declined our invitation for an interview, although Spring Hill did provide the following statement."

The female reporter shifted before beginning to read the nursing home's statement. "We want to express our deepest sympathy to the families of the deceased and will cooperate fully with all authorities and regulators to determine exactly how this tragic event happened. It is our mission to ensure nothing like this ever takes place again."

The abstract statement did nothing to ease Carrie's troubled thoughts. She hardly slept that night. Or the night after. Over the next week, her compulsion to follow post-hurricane reports grew — and with it, a thickening fog of fatigue enveloped her. It took ever-flowing coffee and a lot of self-talk to push through. But in addition to her chronic tiredness, an inner anger was growing inside Carrie as well.

At home alone, Carrie would sometimes rage about the hurricane and those she felt were at fault for neglect and abuse. In other instances, she blamed herself, wondering how many had tried to call for help when she and her co-workers were unable to do their jobs. Her emotions peaked during one of her work shifts.

Carrie mentally identified the caller as a whiner within seconds. Compared to the people who really needed help, the elderly and mentally challenged people who had suffered needlessly, this person did not have a problem. *Lady, who cares if they want to charge you for extra ranch dressing?*

The cynical statement nearly slipped out of Carrie's mouth. And in that moment, where a single mistake could have meant losing her job, the light came on for Carrie.

She realized her opinions, thoughts, judgements, and feelings about things she had absolutely no control over, were not going to change anything or make bad situations any better. In reality, Carrie knew if she did not get a handle on herself, those inner reflections were going to make things worse, and possibly even cost someone their life. At the very least, Carrie's wild emotions could endanger the career she had worked so hard for. Carrie's compulsive activity was affecting her ability to conduct herself in a truly professional manner.

The first decision Carrie made was not to turn the television on and to turn off her news app notifications. She battled a healthy dose of withdrawal during the first forty-eight hours, but distracting herself with nourishing diversions helped occupy her mind.

Carrie took up brisk walking, and at the prompting of a friend, began using essential oils aromatherapy to soothe her nerves. It surprised her to discover how powerful exercise and scent were in helping melt stress away. She also found a person she felt safe confiding in, and revealed her secret turmoil. It was not someone she worked with or even knew.

Carrie called a trusted resource agency and found out there were people trained to help women and men in emergency services fields like her. She connected immediately with the woman on the other end of the line, and felt instantly relieved to realize she was not the first person to struggle this way. Carrie breathed easier knowing she was not alone.

It took months for Carrie to learn how to let go of her guilt, her pre-judgements, and to simply do her job, but eventually, she regained her foundational balance. Four months after her inner wake-up and many phone calls to her resource mentor later, Carrie braved a conversation with her supervisor.

Instead of the repercussions she feared, Carrie was surprised to learn there was an interest in providing an in-house resource program for their entire team to access. Carrie's conversation became a catalyst for implementing a monthly group chat — where you could talk about anything job related. Within a year, Carrie's 9-1-1 co-workers had built stronger bonds and became a more cohesive group. No news drama exhilaration could compare with Carrie's newfound sense of true belonging.

### Profiling Carrie's Reactions

Every human being filters facts through their feelings — even if they don't grasp that truth. Past history often predicts reactions to present day situations. People don't always recognize their triggers, so it's important to ask, *Why am I feeling this way?*, or, *What is this reminding me of?*, when strong emotions overtake them.

In Carrie's situation, it wasn't until something more dramatic spotlighted her propensity for judgment, leading to risky consequences, that she recognized her pattern of making hasty decisions, before gathering all of the facts.

## Questions to Consider

- **Why do you think this disaster hit Carrie differently than others that occurred before?**
- **How do assumptions, pre-conceived opinions, and too-quick judgments cause issues on the job?**
- **What is it that makes us view other people's mistakes as being condemnation worthy, while expecting people to understand external factors and show mercy for our errors?**

## C.O.D.E. Conduct

**Communication** — If you believe it's safe, try confiding any confusing, fearful, or chaotic feelings to someone in leadership. However, you must use caution before venting to just anyone. Due diligence is called for, to ensure you are speaking to someone who provides a safe place for you to land.

**Objectiveness** — When your own feelings overwhelm or baffle you, try the facts versus feelings exercise. Take a piece of paper and draw a vertical line down the middle. On one side write *Facts*, and list every verifiable piece of evidence you can associate with the situation disturbing you. On the other side of the paper, write *Feelings*. Now list every emotion you feel about the circumstance(s) you are dealing with. This simple process often brings great clarity to confusion.

**Dedication** — Determine to listen and weigh the facts before jumping to conclusions. And even if you are clear on someone else's wrong-doing, remind yourself that your job is not to judge or condemn others.

**Engagement** — Guard yourself against pulling away from other people when you are upset. Instinct says hide what you are struggling with, but the more alone we feel, the more our minds entertain dangerous thoughts, strange imaginations, and off-balance illusions. Often, when we talk about what we feel, we discover a more balanced and healthier view of the facts. At the very least, just venting the emotional gunk, brings relief.

## EMT/Paramedic Summary

Paramedics or EMT's are usually the first healthcare professionals to arrive at an accident or emergency scene. A paramedic is usually one of a small ambulance crew who assesses the situation and determines the appropriate treatment to be given to the victim, prior to sending them on to the hospital. Decisions require quick actions, followed through in a calculated manner. Paramedics must be well-trained and possess exceptional people skills, because some of the people they deal with are difficult to manage.

EMS professionals are often screamed at, treated rudely, and even endure physical abuse when victims and bystanders are influenced by alcohol, drugs, shock, or their adrenalin charged emotions.

Now, they must also incorporate Tactical Emergency Combat Care principles and practices into their areas of expertise. We can no longer believe that terror events are isolated to a particular community or situation — they can and will happen when we are not expecting them, in places and circumstances that are difficult, if not impossible, to predict. The first-line responders who do battle to save and protect are the women and men who wear the EMS uniform. Pressure can take its toll on the best-trained individuals.

Another ongoing fight they wage is for a balanced personal life. Since a paramedic or EMT can be called on any time. They work many nights and weekends. Their social life suffers. While the rest of the world sleeps, they are often taking care of people — emergencies don't wait for convenient hours.

Fortunately, EMS workers are trained, equipped, and prepared to cope with every aspect of the job, and the fulfillment of what they do can offset the strains they feel. Most people are not capable of the heroic abilities EMS responders display on a daily basis.

This section is dedicated to the brave, front line warriors who run into situations most people run away from. We are thankful you continue to fight the good fight for the helpless, defenseless, and weak. Thank you!

# Chapter 9
# A Cluttered Mind

Cen-Com interrupted Joe's studies again. "I'm never going to pass my final certification exam," he complained as he shut his paramedic training manual.

"Hustle up. Duty calls," Shannon yelled from the ambulance.

Two minutes later, Shannon shoved the van into reverse, threw the lights and sirens on, then gunned it while Joe shook his head. *He's going to get us killed on our way to try and save lives.* Joe looked at his watch, *1615 hours.*

As soon as the ambulance pulled up to the residence, Joe and Shannon jumped out simultaneously, rushing to pop the back of the ambulance open. They each snapped on blue Nitrile gloves, then hurriedly grabbed gear and a gurney before jogging toward the home's entrance.

A sheriff's deputy stood at the end of the white gravel drive. "No need to rush, boys. We've got a cadaver, not a live one."

Midway up the steps leading into the mobile home, Joe stopped. He'd hit a thick wall of decomposition.

Shannon bumped into his back. "Hey, what's the hold up?"

Joe turned sideways so his body no longer blocked Shannon's access. His shift partner maneuvered around, and walked past Joe. Shannon obviously didn't inhale right away, but when he did, there was no mistaking it.

He froze. "Whew, that's a ripe one." He waved Joe back into the front position. "As the senior paramedic, I'm making the call, Rookie. You're in the lead on this one, my man."

Joe willed the queasy roll in his stomach to stop. The unequalled stench of human death permeated the trailer, the kind that sticks to your clothes and leaves a film in your mouth, even before you are in full contact with the source. Joe knew the fact that there was no HVAC in operation on a sultry Chicago day heightened the odor and accelerated the decomposition.

Multiple dogs barked and howled from another room, but Joe didn't see them. He did however, see traces that they had been in the room he stood in. He hop-scotched around mounds of animal feces scattered amidst piles of trash and other refuse. As Joe scanned the residence, he noted that the entire home was extremely cluttered and in an extreme state of uncleanliness. Dirt, food and drink stains littered the living room, kitchen, and hallway floors — Joe guessed he would find similar conditions wherever the body lay.

The sheriff's deputy yelled from outside, "He's in the bedroom at the back."

Joe's quest to find the source of death took him down the only path that led from room to room, a single, narrow trail between heaps of debris. At the very end of the hall, he found what he knew awaited him.

A Caucasian male was lying spread eagle at a diagonal angle, across a double bed. He was fully dressed in gray sweatpants, a tattered brown hoodie, and black, no-name tennis shoes.

Joe approached carefully, mentally recalling and reviewing his EMT training as he stepped. The subject's face was bloated, his arms and legs had started to mottle, and purge was observable coming from the mouth and nose area. The victim's abdominal area was bloated and extended due to gas pressure. After checking for a pulse, lividity, and noting the blue tinge on his pallor skin, Joe knew the man had been dead for several hours due to the level of decomposition present. His skin was blistered on areas of his back and upper extremities, and rigor mortis was firmly fixed on all major joints.

There were only two items of interest located near the body, a cigarette lying next to him on the bed and a lighter lying on the floor, centered between his feet. Joe made sure he didn't touch any of the evidence or disturb the scene — from page 43 in his training manual. This was his first death, and he did not want to mess anything up. He thought to himself, *It's one thing to read about a scene, but it's a whole different deal to work one.*

"What've we got?" the coroner made his way through

the maze of excrement to stand near the bed.

Joe didn't know how he should respond. He simply inched back, so the death investigator could complete his job.

The coroner appeared to either not notice or disregard Joe's silence. Speaking his findings out loud into a recorder, he too noted the signs of death and environmental conditions in which the body was found, along with a couple of other details. "It should be noted that the outside temperature reached 91 degrees, and the inside temperature of the mobile home is considerably higher, although exact room temp has not been taken. The entire residence is filled with animal feces, the smell of urine is palpable, and large volumes of trash are scattered and piled everywhere. Cause of death at this time unknown. The body will be taken to the Cook County Medical Examiner's office for autopsy."

When the examination was complete, and the body bagged and loaded into the vehicle, Joe eavesdropped as the sheriff's deputy gave the coroner an update. "I spoke with the person who found the deceased. The victim's name is James Cusamano, and he lives with a woman named...," the deputy tapped his phone to check his notes. "He lives with a Francis Salvador, and she states she knew him to be asleep and snoring at about 1930 hours last evening. Ms. Salvador said as she was leaving for work at approximately 0600 this morning, she heard an alarm sounding in the bedroom. It had shut off, and she assumed Mr. Cusamano was getting up at his normal time. So she left thinking everything was all right."

"Anything else?" the coroner said.

The sheriff continued, "A neighbor stated that he had not seen Mr. Cusamano outside all day. He told me that was not normal."

Back at the station, Joe struggled to dive back into his studies, as his mind ran through the possible reasons for the death of the man he had seen earlier. *Suicide? Not likely as there was no known note, and the evidence on scene did not immediately point to it. Murder? Wouldn't that be something? His first death, a big murder case? Natural causes? Probably, although it wasn't the sexiest scenario. I'll just have to wait for the autopsy report like everyone else.* But waiting would not be easy with Joe's tight work schedule, coupled with his restless spirit over this first death event.

Joe's shifts the rest of the week were quiet, which was a good thing. He was working two other jobs, and his time to study for his certification exam was running out.

The gnawing curiosity over the cause of death of Mr. Cusamano would not go away. His mind would not shut off. Between adrenalin overloads and adrenal fatigue, Joe's brain struggled to process information while his body fought to stay alert. If he could just hold on for two-and-a-half more weeks. Eighteen days. Then he could take his exam, and hopefully pass. It would be easier if he could simply find out how Mr. Cusamano died.

The day of the exam, Joe's nerves were blazing. He felt unprepared, after spending so much emotional and mental energy over the Cusamano case, three jobs, and the constant physical fatigue. But as bad as he felt taking the test, waiting for the results was even worse.

In subsequent weeks, there were days Joe felt like he might have a mental breakdown with all the unknowns in his life, but he had to keep his thoughts and emotions to himself. All three of his jobs required him to appear as if he had everything together — even when he did not. No one wanted a frazzled person administering medical assistance or doing security for major events at the United Center. So Joe wore the mask. The one he didn't yet realize was commonly worn by most who worked in emergency services fields.

Finally, the email he'd waited on arrived. Not realizing he was holding his breath, Joe opened the state educational agency's correspondence. He was relieved to see his passing grade, although he also knew it wasn't up to his full potential. But he'd passed. Joe was a fully-certified paramedic. He was glad no one else was in the room to see him swipe the drops from the edges of his eyes.

Less than a week after Joe received his paramedic certification, he learned the autopsy results of Mr. Cusamano. The man had no injuries or trauma, there was no evidence of anything unusual in his toxicology testing, but the examiner did find coronary heart disease in the victim. The cause of death was ruled, myocardial infarction. The man had died of a heart attack.

Things calmed rather quickly for Joe soon after. He was hired as a paramedic, allowing him to quit one of his three jobs. He could pick and choose events to do security for at the United Center, so he stayed on payroll for side income. Joe also realized how much he'd learned from his first death case — the greatest lesson was the power of avoiding speculation and assumptions.

In hindsight, Joe knew he had lost hours and days while anxiously speculating over the unknown. It could have cost him his dreams and his future. He vowed to never let a cluttered mind plague him again.

## Profiling Joe's Reactions

The mask. Everyone wears one sometimes — there are even seasons and situations that require it. However, if you aren't careful, you can become so skilled at faking it that you forget how to take the mask off. Human beings need safe and appropriate places to be themselves and to have fun, but Joe nearly lost his way in work and studies. He could have become one of the staggering statistics of emergency services workaholics who forget how to live life as a human being.

## Questions to Consider

- **How did Joe's self-talk affect his response to situations?**
- **What could Joe have done to calm his spirit and distract his racing mind?**
- **When was Joe in the most jeopardy due to heavy pressures coming from multiple sources?**

## C.O.D.E. Conduct

**Communication** — What you say to yourself matters as much as what you say to others — maybe more so. People convince themselves of many things, based on mindless conversations with themselves. Pay attention to the messages playing in your head, and don't convince yourself that feelings are actually facts.

**Objectiveness** — Remember that fatigue, dehydration, hunger, and pressure-cooker stress influences how people view you. If you are worn out and worn down, you are not in the best position to think impartially.

**Dedication** — No matter how busy you are, devote yourself to periodic mental breaks. These don't necessarily require a lot of time, but they can energize and clear your mind of emotional clutter. Take sixty seconds and visualize yourself relaxing in your favorite outdoor setting. Run in place, or do some other aerobic activity for sixty seconds. Breathe slowly, in and out, for sixty seconds. Even if you have to hide in the restroom for an extra minute to get the reset you need, take it. You will do a better job if you give yourself a moment to relax.

**Engagement** — Engage in at least one healthy extra-curricular activity outside of work, preferably something fun. An adventure hobby, a resting activity, a stimulating exercise, or a regular night out with friends where laughter is the self-medication. Avoid alcohol.

## Chapter 10
## An Empty Gut

Terry Jordan walked past the empty room and tried not to think about the loneliness it represented. She couldn't help peeking in before continuing down the hall. *I can't believe he's been gone four months. I pray you're okay today, Baby.*

She sighed and pushed off of the door frame to force herself into the kitchen. After rummaging through the refrigerator, Terry finally settled on an egg. She had to push the carton of black cherry yogurt aside to reach the turkey, bacon, and avocado she wanted. She didn't have the heart to pitch the yogurt, though it was long past its expiration date. *I know I should throw this away, but it's Dalton's favorite.*

Terry prepared her breakfast and sat at the counter to eat. Alone. Again.

Her eighteen-year-old son had left her to take on the world — seeking adventure, fortune, and his own special place to fit in. Sadly, the way he'd left had broken his mother's heart.

At least Terry had work to keep her mind occupied.

Three-and-a-half hours later, she was on shift, and for a moment had forgotten her troubles. She laughed with her co-workers at a silly joke, until Cen-Com interrupted their moment of lightheartedness.

Terry hopped in the emergency vehicle, but guilt flooded her mind on the drive. *How dare I laugh, when I don't know where Dalton is?*

When they arrived at the address, the reason for the 9-1-1 call became immediately obvious.

A young woman, who looked to be approximately twenty years of age, bulged with pregnancy. The floor beneath her feet was covered in blood.

Terry made it to her first. "Ma'am, we need to get you off your feet."

"My babies. Please save my babies. I need a hospital."

Terry waved the gurney close. "Yes ma'am. And we're here to take you there. But right now, we need you to lie

97

down. Just relax, and we'll help you."

"Okay," the woman said as she allowed Terry and the other paramedic to support her arms, while gently moving her into a flat position.

Terry calmed the woman by asking questions to distract her while they did their work. "What's your name?"

"Maria."

"You're doing great, Maria. Now, did you say babies? As in more than one?"

The young woman giggled. "Yeah. I was having twins. Boys."

Terry noted the past tense statement. *Fear? Or subconscious slip?*

She drove the thoughts from her mind. It wasn't her job to figure it out, but Terry knew she needed to tell the appropriate person when she saw them.

Six minutes after their arrival, Terry and her partner wound their way through street and stoplights, sirens wailing. Though she had lost some blood, the patient was stable, but her fetuses were not fairing as well.

At the hospital, Terry and her co-worker turned their patient over to the emergency room staff. There was nothing more they could do at this point, except wait to hear how things turned out. As a mother herself, Terry's heart went out to the woman whose boys were in jeopardy. Especially with the emptiness in her soul, since her own child had cut off contact. There was no pain like that of a missing child.

The next day, on her own time, Terry went to the hospital to get an update. She spoke to the attending OB physician. But what she heard brought no peace — in actuality, it raised her memory and a red flag.

The attending's face softened with a look of sadness as she spoke. "The fetuses were at a twenty-nine week gestation. The woman delivered Baby A as a live birth this morning, but it was not able to sustain life. She had a strong heart rate, but could not support respirations. We delivered Baby B via C section immediately following, due to a nonreassuring fetal heart rate. We worked with Baby B from the time of his birth at 1836 hours until 1958 hours, when he was pronounced dead." The doctor paused before continuing. "We almost lost the mother, too. She had a sudden and drastic drop in blood pressure due to excessive bleeding. Thankfully, she's out of the woods now."

Terry spoke cautiously. "Doctor, the mother said something as we were loading her on the gurney for transport. Something I think you should know."

"Oh?"

"She referred to her babies in past tense. Maybe it's nothing, but I almost had the sense she knew they weren't going to make it."

The doctor scowled. "We've already scheduled an autopsy on both fetuses, as a matter of protocol. I've secured the placenta for the medical examiner as well. They'll run an advanced toxicology panel, so if there's something to this, the tests will reveal it. Unfortunately, nothing would surprise me. But it's too early to know, and assuming will do nothing more than make matters worse."

"You're right. Thank you for that perspective." It was one Terry needed for more than the situation at hand.

At home that night, Terry thought back to her life with Dalton. Their relationship had been tumultuous — even since his conception. She'd considered an abortion when his father walked out at the news of her pregnancy. Back then, Terry couldn't imagine how she would make it on her own with an extra mouth to feed. But she wasn't able to follow through with the termination of her baby — a decision she still felt deeply grateful for, even though the situation with her son wasn't what she wanted it to be.

Terry instinctively picked up her phone and texted him again. *Hey Babe, I'm not trying to bug you, just wanted you to know I love and miss you. Hope to hear from you soon.*

By the time Terry went to bed, there was still no response — as usual.

The next evening, fresh off her shift, Terry had just settled on the couch to watch her favorite TV show with a bowl of popcorn and a glass of wine, when the call came in.

"Ms. Jordan, this is Dr. Graham. We spoke about the woman whose twin fetuses died."

"Yes, Doctor. I remember. Are the autopsy results in?"

"They are, but the news isn't good. We found traces of the synthetic prostaglandin drug, Misoprostol in the tissues of the fetuses and in the placenta. It's a cheap prescription used to treat gastric ulcers. But it's also a common self-induced abortion choice for some women, especially those in the Latino culture here in New York. I'm sure the drastic loss of blood and drop in Maria's blood pressure were a direct result of the Misoprostol in her system. She's fortunate she didn't hemorrhage and bleed out, like many of the women who try this method for terminating their pregnancies. Too bad her babies weren't as fortunate. We called the deaths into the Child Abuse and Neglect Hotline. The authorities will take it from here."

Terry cried as they hung up. A myriad of emotions swamped her mind and spirit, all swirling together with thoughts of her son. The phone call triggered fresh fears and sadness over Dalton's absence.

In a matter of minutes, Terry slid from the couch cushion and crumpled on the floor in front it. *I would give anything for another chance with him.* The thought drove her into a powerful round of hyperventilating sobs.

Twenty minutes later, Terry's gut felt empty. She doubted there were any tears left to shed, as she hiccuped the last of her ugly cry away. Her emotions finally simmered down enough for her to breathe normally.

*I have so many regrets.* Terry wiped her nose with the back of her hand and sniffled.

She thought of the young woman who discarded her babies. *I wonder if Maria regrets what she did and wishes she had another chance to do things over.* A huge wave of anger swamped her soul. *How could she kill her own babies?* But then, Terry remembered. *I almost took Dalton's life before he had a chance to live it.*

Terry wrestled anger and guilt through most of the night. At least she had the next day off.

When she woke up, Terry needed something extra to help with her wine headache. She decided to walk to the Blue Bottle Coffee shop for a splurge of the strong, black brew.

While waiting for her drink, a pamphlet lying on the floor near the counter caught Terry's eye. Deciding not to leave the litter for someone else to pick up, she bent down.

In simple red letters, it read, *Avail: A Safe Place for Confident Decisions*. She opened the brochure, and the coincidence was not lost on Terry. She was holding an ad for a pregnancy resource center.

Terry's first instinct was to throw the document in the trash, but something held her back. She tucked it in her purse before grabbing her coffee off the counter and heading back to her apartment. Once home, she tossed the pamphlet on the end table by her couch.

The brochure rested there, untouched for three weeks. But every time Terry saw it, something inside her stirred, especially when she thought of Dalton, or the reasons a mother might feel desperate enough to abort her unborn children. After a lot of soul searching, Terry knew she could have easily been a Maria — maybe choosing a different way of going about it, but resulting in the same sad outcome.

Finally, Terry picked up the phone. She spoke briefly with someone at Avail about coming for a tour. Terry didn't explain that she had more than a tour in mind.

When she'd seen and heard what Avail had to offer, Terry was convinced she'd made the right decision in coming. She needed a purpose to help take her mind off the throbbing ache from her child's absence. Terry signed up as a volunteer right away.

The required training inspired Terry even more, and she soon looked forward to her weekly work at the pregnancy resource center. Many Marias came and went, some still choosing differently than Terry hoped they would, but others opted to carry their children to term. They either raised them or gave them to a loving family who had prayed for a child to adopt.

At Avail, there was no pressure in what a woman chose. The agency only provided fully informed education and counsel. The saddest women who came through however, were haunted by a choice they couldn't take back, and were reeling from the after-effects. Terry ached for them most of all.

Though her role did not come in the form of any advisement, Terry knew she and others were making a positive impact in the lives of the women who came through the center's doors. Mostly, they listened, and that was often enough.

Terry was amazed when her four-year volunteer anniversary arrived. *How did it go so fast?* The celebration made her smile, Avail, along with the work she loved as a paramedic, helped fill the emptiness she felt in her gut. There was only one, very important thing missing in her life. With the image of Dalton's face in her mind, she prayed as she often did. *Lord, continue to keep my child safe, and when the time is right, bring him back into my life. Amen.*

That night, Terry nestled onto her couch with a glass of Ginger Ale and her favorite snack — popcorn. She turned on the TV to stream the next episode of her favorite show, when her phone pinged.

Terry started to ignore it, frustrated that her moment of peace was interrupted. But curiosity got the best of her. She picked up the phone.

Seeing the message brought a downpour of tears from a well of bottled-up emotions. Terry had to read the text numerous times before her brain would fully register what the words said.

Dalton had finally messaged back. "Mom, is it ok if I come home? I'm sorry. I love u."

Terry couldn't type the word *yes* fast enough. After several transmissions back and forth, Dalton told her he would arrive in a couple of hours. Suddenly, Terry was off the floor and dancing on her couch like a little kid.

The last bit of emptiness in her filled to overflowing. All was right with her world — Terry's boy was coming home.

Dalton's return wasn't a fairy tale. There were bumps and setbacks, but mother and son worked through them, repeatedly choosing to love, even when they agreed to disagree. Plus, Dalton had grown up while on his own. It took adjusting for Terry to realize he was no longer a little boy, and did not need his mom to run his life. She learned to respect that — and saw how her regret over Dalton's missing father had caused her to overcompensate — leading to her son's fight for independence.

As they worked through their differences, Terry's paramedic job and continuing work as a volunteer gave her purpose, taught her how to interact more objectively with her son, and helped her release Dalton to pursue his own passions. Terry freed her child from the trap of her own guilt-induced desires and expectations. As they worked their way through an adult mother/son relationship, they got to know each other better and their bond deepened. The lessons were hard-earned, but provided Terry with even more encouragements to share with others like her.

### Profiling Terry's Reactions

Conflict comes from a single word — expectation. We either expect something from a person who can't or doesn't deliver, or our expectations are met, but we fail to express appreciation, making the person who delivered feel as if their actions were rejected.

At first, Terry didn't realize her subconscious expectations of her son were pushing him away. Neither did she understand she was projecting an expectation on the young woman, Maria, and others like her. Obsessing over broken relationships won't fix them — instead, it actually deepens the emptiness inside our guts. However, when we release our expectations, listen, and are willing to learn, often the brokenness heals itself.

### Questions to Consider

- **What impact did Terry's expectations have on her personal and professional relationships?**
- **Why do you think volunteering at the pregnancy resource center helped Terry deal with her pain?**
- **When is facing emotions helpful? When, if ever, can it be harmful?**

## C.O.D.E. Conduct

**Communication** — Listening is as important a part of communication as anything we speak. You have two ears and one mouth, so practice listening twice as much as you speak and prepare yourself for what you will learn at work and at home.

**Objectiveness** — We often believe we are acting objectively, but lose sight of how past events steer our current emotional perspectives. Pay attention to your own reactions, strong responses are usually driven by emotion.

**Dedication** — Giving a segment of your time, energy, and talents to helping others is a proven depression-buster. Anyone working in emergency fields is prone to this insidious funk. But *studies show when you focus on others, and dedicate yourself to a greater good through a different environment, your mood lifts and you can deal with hardships much better — whether they occur at work or home.

**Engagement** — "Be present in the moment." This message is much more than cliché, and it's not a New Age mantra, so be careful not to tune it out. There is deep value to plugging in to what's going on around you in the present moment. If nothing else, your mind is occupied so it can't feel depressed about the past or anxious about the future. Get involved, fully involved, with the people, activities, and places in your experience now.

# Chapter 11
# Double Dose High

"Are you serious, Chalmers?" Beth said, when her partner relayed the address just called in.

"Serious as an overdose."

Beth rolled her eyes at Tim's off-handed joke, as well as at the source of the call. "This is the third time this month. It would serve him right if he didn't pull out of it this time," she said.

"Whoa, that's harsh. You're usually the compassionate one," Tim said.

Beth turned the key in the ignition and started the ambulance. "You're right. I just get so tired of treating a person who obviously doesn't care if he lives or dies. It seems like a waste for us to care more about his existence than he does." She'd barely finished her sentence when they pulled into the driveway of the residence.

A scraggly looking blonde in dirty pajamas with matted hair and a pockmarked face, jumped up and down waving her arms.

As soon as Beth opened the door, the girl's screams assaulted her — full frontal. "He's inside. You've got to save him. Hurry. Eric's dying."

A tinge of a smile played at the edges of the girl's mouth, telling the truth of her emotional state.

*I know the game*, Beth thought. *Timing a fix of heroin that could kill you with a call to 9-1-1. Get us here just in time to shock you back to life with a hit of Narcan®, then you get the double dose high from the drug, coupled with the euphoria of cheating death at the last moment.* Beth moved briskly past the young woman, swinging her medical bag to the other hand so she wouldn't bump the hysterical girl. *I don't want to play this Russian Roulette game with you and Eric Chalmers. I'm tired of it. You'd better feel grateful that I'm a professional.* Beth walked inside the house. Regardless of the reason for the call, she had an obligation to uphold.

But the situation didn't unfold how Beth expected.

Eric Chalmers lay in a spreading pool of vomit, his skin ashen and blotched. His body was contorted, although it lay completely still. From appearance, he must have stopped convulsing several minutes earlier. Not a good sign. As Beth looked at Eric Chalmers' graying body, she thought, *You may have played your game one too many times.*

Beth and Tim knelt on the floor. Beth popped the vial of Narcan®, like she'd done for Eric Chalmers during a dozen calls before. This one final time, it didn't work.

When Eric pulled the trigger to play Russian Roulette, a fatal bullet was in the chamber. No amount of Narcan® could save him now. And Beth would have to live with her guilt.

They drove to the hospital in silence, with Eric's cooling body in the back. Beth wished she could turn the radio on and blast her thoughts away to block out memories of her uncaring words about a young man who may have been a fool, but who was still a person worth saving. For the first time in her life, Beth wanted to turn the hands of time back a couple of hours. But she couldn't forget the awful things she'd said about Eric Chalmers. And her calloused words would replay in her dreams for many nights to come — along with a haunting question. *Who have I become?*

Her mood did not improve following another overdose death the next week, especially when she overheard some of her co-workers. She didn't like that their voices resurrected her guilt.

*We've all done it.* Beth tried to reassure herself as she sat silently in the middle of the bench seat, sandwiched between Greg's and Lila's bantering.

Greg was complaining about the latest young man who had lost his life to heroin. "I don't know what these idiots are thinking. They inject this stuff into their veins, they ingest God knows what, and then they cry wolf, expecting us to come rescue them from the willful messes they create."

Lila countered, "It does get old."

"We've got real patients who need us, while we waste our time on fools." Greg said.

"I get tired of dealing with them too, but that's kind of harsh, don't you think?" Lila sighed nervously.

Beth kept her thoughts to herself. *How do we become so jaded? Two weeks ago, I may not have said what I thought out loud like Greg and Lila, but my attitude would have mirrored theirs. I became a paramedic to help save lives, not to pronounce judgments on those who lose theirs.*

Three days later, Greg's own perspective shifted.

When Beth and Lila pulled into the driveway of their second call of the day, they were both surprised to find Greg inside the residence. Crying.

A teenage boy with dark, wavy hair lay in an all too familiar position. Vomit. Foam in the mouth. Pock marks. Loss of skin color.

Greg's eyes were glazed when he looked at Beth and Lila. "He's my nephew. My sister's son. I held him the day he was born. I thought he'd kicked it. He said he'd kicked it. My sister believed him, but she has to, she's his mom. I should have known better. Now it's too late, he's one of the idiots now."

"Where's your sister?" Beth said as she knelt to take the

boy's vitals.

"She's on her way back. She had to go out of town on business. She asked me to check in on Robby while she was gone. I brought him breakfast." Greg pointed to a bagel bag on the counter. "I brought him breakfast."

The next few months were somber at the paramedic station. Beth attempted to hide her inner feelings, though the mask didn't cover as much as she hoped. Day after day, she silently contemplated her guilt while Greg mourned outwardly the loss of his nephew Robby. Everyone walked on eggshells around them, afraid to crush what was left of their fragile spirits.

For Beth, an unexpected meeting triggered the beginning of her healing — a chance encounter in a laundromat. Or *was* it by chance?

She had just snapped a white towel to fold it when a man with a nice, ordinary face approached with a sheepish smile. "I hate to bother you, but the change machine is broken, and I need another dollar's worth of quarters. You wouldn't have any you could spare, would you?"

"Sure," Beth said.

They chatted over agitating clothes.

"Do you work in the area?" the man asked.

"I'm a paramedic. You?"

The man's eyebrows lifted. "I've always admired people who work in your field. It takes an honorable person to do what you do."

Beth's shoulders slumped. "I'm not that honorable."

"I can tell by looking at you that you're honorable. I'm a pastor, I know these things." He winked.

"You're a pastor? Can I ask you a question?"

He chuckled. "Sure."

"I think I've done something unforgivable. We had a

patient, a young kid. He was a heroine user and an habitual 9-1-1 caller. We went there at least twice a month. He would take the drugs, call us, and count on a hit of Narcan to pull him out. Only he tried it one too many times. We lost him a few weeks ago."

"I'm so sorry," the pastor said compassionately.

"But on that last call, I didn't want to go. I was mad at the guy for calling. So you see, I'm not an honorable person. What kind of paramedic does that?"

A look of compassion crossed the pastor's face. "A human one. You didn't want him to die."

"But I said some things. Terrible things. I'm not honorable, I'm awful."

The pastor turned to face Beth fully. "Listen, you are not awful. You are human. God is willing to forgive you, but you need to forgive yourself."

"How could God forgive me? In essence, I wished my patient dead."

"You did not make the choices for that young man that put his life in jeopardy. You took the call, didn't you?"

"Yes."

"You did everything within your power to save him. Right?"

"Yes." Tears ran off Beth's chin.

"Then you did the best you could. God will forgive you. All you have to do is ask. And if you decide you are unforgivable, then you are saying you know more than the One who created you."

"I never thought about it that way. Thank you, Pastor."

That night, as Beth lay in bed, she looked up to the ceiling. "God, I'll be honest with you. I'm not sure if you really exist, but if you do, then will you forgive me? And teach me how to forgive myself? I guess that's it for now. I don't really know how to do this prayer thing, but if you're there, thanks for listening. Amen. I think that's what I'm supposed to say."

Oddly, Beth had the first full night's sleep she'd had since her guilt had consumed her. Greg however, didn't fare so well. Though Beth had spoken to him multiple times about her meeting with the pastor and how it had changed her outlook, he didn't want to hear about it. He also refused counseling from his superiors or licensed professionals. Greg had quit within six months, but only after he posted this note on social media:

*Stop Dying!*

*Dispatch sends us out for cardiac arrest. Mentally, we prepare as we drive to the scene. We think about equipment need, and start figuring out who will grab what bags when we land on scene. Our lead EMT reads the notes on the computer out loud, "Twenty-two-year-old female. Not breathing. CPR started."*

*Anxiety sticks in all of our guts, and we think the worst — but no one dares speak it.*

*Two police cars, a medic, and fire truck all arrive at the same time we do, as if orchestrated on purpose. Five of us storm the front door simultaneously, equipment and meds in hand.*

*The wails and cries of the family assault us as soon as we step inside. "No! Why?" They repeat the same exclamations over and over.*

*We find you in your room. You still have a teddy bear on the bed, posters of celebrities on your wall, dried flowers in a vase, probably from a homecoming or prom, and pictures of friends on your dresser. We also see your beer can, next to a syringe, needle, spoon, and lighter.*

*You are crumpled on the floor, dressed in soft, pink pajama bottoms and a faded sweatshirt that reads, Hollister. You look relaxed. We are not.*

*We start assessing you. No pulse. No breath. Though you are cold to the touch, none of us want to give up on you.*

*Decision time. What do we do next?*

*We grab our box of Narcan. The room is oddly quiet as we all look to the lead medic, wondering silently what our next step should be.*

*She looks up from her monitor, checking for any heart activity. She shakes her head.*

*Without saying anything, we all begin the motions. Before, we rushed, in hopes of saving you — now we move slowly, starting the equipment clean up. The medic calls the coroner. Though we are as silent as you are still, in our heads, we are all screaming, cursing, and crying. Like your family we wonder, why.*

*You are a daughter, sister, granddaughter, aunt, niece, friend, neighbor, and co-worker. You have 1,021 Facebook friends. You also had a secret. Now we all know it, but it is too late. The addiction monster won. Why did you ever give him the first shot at stealing your life? Why didn't you pass, when the first hit was offered? So many whys.*

*As we exit your bedroom, we walk past your family. Through sniffles, they're talking to the police, trying to get details about your last known moments, before death took you away.*

*From the kitchen, a soft, toddler voice asks, "Is Mommy all right?"*

*This is too much. Now we are not just screaming, cursing, and crying silently. We can't hold back the tears. They stream down our faces as we drive back to the station — in utter silence.*

*Why, precious girl, did you not dial, 1-800-662-HELP or some other person who might help you? Because you said yes to the monster one more time, we are all wrecked.*

Though Greg could see the need for the addicted to seek help, he could not pick up the phone for himself. Instead, he struggled alone, trying to overcome his own guilt, and he refused to allow forgiveness to heal his hurting heart. All Beth could do was pray for Greg and hope he would someday find the peace that had somehow visited her that day.

## Profiling Beth's Reactions

It's easy to join in gossip, make fun of people, or slip into a tainted and pessimistic view of others — all of us have done it. Human beings are often soured by the mundane, the repetitive, or what appears to be a waste of time, but when you work in emergency services, each time may be the crucial moment for saving or losing a life. No matter what the people you're treating have done, they are human and worth your best efforts.

When Beth thought about the mistakes she'd made, and the grace extended to her, it helped renew her inner compassion. Balanced professional objectivity made her more effective on the job.

## Questions to Consider

- **When you think about the epidemic of people playing with death, how does it make you feel?**
- **What history, circumstances, or secrets might cause someone to choose chemical substances to smother their pain?**
- **Why do you think Beth was able to forgive when Greg could not?**

## C.O.D.E. Conduct

**Communication** — Consider conversation starters. What will give you the courage to face your feelings and vent them to people who may be able to help you work through your tangled feelings?

- In these kinds of situations, I feel. . . .
- One particular scene caused me to think. . . .
- Have you ever dealt with. . . .

**Objectiveness** — Consider the S.W.O.T. analysis when facing difficult emotions from a dramatic scene or series of challenging cases. What are the strengths, weaknesses, opportunities, and threats this exposure presents for you?

**Dedication** — All humans use coping mechanisms — some choose exercise, nutritious foods, aromatherapy from essential oils, or a myriad of other healthy options, while others choose destructive means like laziness, over-eating, shopping, inappropriate sex, alcohol, drugs, etc. Before making rash judgments, consider the unknown facts you may not be aware of, regarding the people you meet and treat.

**Engagement** — Forgive yourself for making mistakes and being human. And on a practical note, as you drive away from an especially difficult crisis scene, provide yourself with a soothing environment in your vehicle. It could be a certain form of music, a scent that reminds you of someone special, a favorite food flavor that takes you back to a happy time in your life, a picture of a special vacation spot, or the sensation of a comforting piece of fabric. Healthy engagement can spare you from making unhealthy decisions.

## Chapter 12
## Prescribed Addiction

"Right behind you," Keith said to George, his shift partner — then he popped the ibuprofen into his mouth. He had a raging headache.

"Get a move on," George said. "You don't want to be late on your first big day. Vegas is waiting, my man."

But Keith could not have known what he would see on scene.

They arrived within seconds of law enforcement.

Before entering the room, one of the officers warned them, "She's breathing, but barely hanging on. Prepare yourself, boys. It's one of the ugliest things I've ever had to look at." He brushed his eye, like he was attempting to remove an irritant. "I know you have to do what's necessary to save her, but try not to disturb the evidence. We need to preserve what we can. It's definitely a crime scene. But take care of the girl first."

The savagery committed against the young, dark-haired woman laying on the floor defied description. Keith's mind could hardly process what his eyes were telling him.

Her face, turned sideways, was broken, purple, puffed, and blackened. Her wrists and ankles were bound with white zip ties, while her arms and legs were covered in deep lacerations. A bloodied X was cut into the woman's left shoulder and another covered her entire buttocks.

As Keith stepped fully into the room, an officer was pulling a damp, rainbow colored sock from the woman's mouth. Her respirations were so faint, it wasn't until Keith and George knelt down to begin their assessments that they confirmed she was alive. She neither moved or whimpered, when they gently rolled her nude and contorted body from her stomach to her back. Blood trickled from multiple wounds spanning the top of her head, covering her stomach, across her thighs, and down to her toes.

Though her backside was covered in crimson, the pressure on her front had reduced the amount of blood flow in those areas. Now, Keith could see her full facial features, and he wasn't prepared for what they appeared to reveal.

Even though there was extensive damage to the woman's tissue and bones, Keith was struck by familiarity. He froze. *Tina? Please God, don't let it be Tina.*

George voiced Keith's fears. "Oh, my God. Is this your fiancée?"

To Keith, it sounded like George's muffled question echoed from a deep well dug into dry ground. Keith tried to respond, but his body refused to cooperate.

Several seconds later, Keith realized George was shouting at him. "Keith. Snap out of it. I understand, but I need you to pay attention. Whoever this is, she needs us. Keith!"

"Sorry," Keith spoke while moving his hands to assist his partner. "Do we have a name? Do we know who she is?" Both paramedics continued to work on the woman, but in auto-pilot fashion, as they glanced toward the two detectives who were watching intently from the door frame.

One of the police officers spoke up. "According to the mail on the table by her front door, her name is Ginny Bronson."

A warm rush of adrenal relief flooded Keith and infused him with the energy he needed to kick into high gear. As they worked on the young woman, Keith stayed calm and professional. . . until they delivered her to the hospital.

The attending trauma physician called Ginny Bronson's death at 14:22. She'd been raped, severely beaten, and stabbed seventeen times. She was only twenty-five-years-old. And she bore a striking likeness to his fiancée, Tina.

Without hands-on work to keep his mind busy, plus finding out the extent of the woman's injuries, the force of all Keith's emotions erupted physically. He walked briskly outside to vomit beside the building. He would not forget his first day as an EMT, no matter how much time passed.

Six years later, Keith still saw images of Tina's doppelgänger from time to time. If he was especially tired or had a rough shift, when he laid down to rest, his mind imagined the brutality of Ginny's torture. His brain replayed the moment she was rolled over, when Keith came face-to-face with a fear he didn't expect. That day had almost cost him everything.

In his first weeks as a new paramedic, Keith had worked hard to wear a look of composure. Sometimes, he even fooled himself, but never for long. The days passed, but the mask became heavier — especially as his anxiety over his fiancée's well-being increased.

Occasionally on the drive home, Keith lost his composure, sometimes so much so, that he had to pull the car over and stop. In other instances, he snapped or lashed out at people for minor inconveniences or misunderstandings. Yet, Keith didn't always understand what was happening inside himself or why. It might have seemed obvious to others, if they had had any clue about his struggles — but he was committed to hiding his fearful feelings. And he never connected the homicide to his outbursts.

One day, he injured his knee jumping into the ambulance. Keith soon realized however, the prescription painkillers helped more than his knee.

Keith started self-medicating before the three-month anniversary of Ginny Bronson's death. It helped dull the pain, at least temporarily. But he still couldn't tame the constant worry for his fiancée.

Thinking marriage would fix his obsessive fear for Tina's safety, Keith insisted they move their wedding date up. His fiancée said, "Yes," with utter excitement. She did not understand the underlying reason for the suggestion.

The compulsion to protect escalated before the honeymoon ended. Marriage did not solve Keith's problems. Things worsened after they got home.

As much as he hated his anxiety, he hated the impact on his relationship with Tina most. Since the murder, every area of their lives together was tainted.

Keith hated walking in the door to hear his wife ask, "How are you?" He wished she'd quit asking.

When she begged him to talk to her, he shut down, opting instead for another pain pill.

Keith wore his feelings of helplessness and shame like an invisible cloak. Day after day, he found it harder to do his job and even harder to hide his emotional and physical issues from Tina.

The weeks turned into years, and eventually, Tina stopped asking how he was. Nine days before their sixth anniversary, after finding yet another prescribed narcotics bottle from one of the multiple doctors he'd conned into feeding his dependency, Tina left. Keith knew he deserved her rejection.

After he'd rebuffed her many attempts to support him, Keith didn't feel worthy of his wife, so he made no attempt to fight. Sadly, he didn't realize until it was far too late. Fighting for her was precisely what his wife wanted.

When Keith knew he was on the verge of losing his paramedic's position, he followed a familiar pattern — find another department in another county who needed a spot filled, then quit before they could fire him. Between the divorce, his financial ruin, and his increasing need for more and more painkillers, Keith's latest position would be his last in the field.

When his house of carefully stacked cards fell, it forced Keith to take a hard look in the mirror. He wouldn't find out why until a few more years passed and he underwent intensive counseling. After uncovering the true origin of his pain, healing could begin.

Once he'd gone through therapy himself, Keith had become a certified counselor for those working in emergency services fields. His heart, passion, and background, made him especially effective, while allowing him to stay connected to the brother and sisterhood he cared so much about.

Keith told his story often. "I was young and didn't understand what was happening to me. I didn't seek any kind of help. I rode a roller coaster between not eating enough and binging. I abused my own body, mind, and spirit. I ran everyone I cared about away. And when I closed my eyes to try and sleep, the flashbacks and nightmares consumed me.

I lost my wife, my home, and car, I lost my jobs, and I

nearly lost my life. I tried to drown it all in prescription painkillers. It wasn't until I gave in to brokenness that I found myself. When I received a professional diagnosis of post-traumatic stress disorder, it was like someone turned the light on in my dark world. I suddenly knew I wasn't insane or crazy. I was reacting normally to an abnormal kind of stress. I used to think PTSD was a military thing. Now I know it affects emergency responders and everyday people, too. We all fight our own wars. Some even lose their lives.

In an article published by ems1.com on February 6, 2017, titled, *Mental Illness Treatment: Hope for EMS Providers*, it is reported that 'thirty-seven percent of EMS workers reported having suicidal thoughts and five percent reported having attempted suicide.' Suicide is one of the greatest killers of those in our field."

Keith's passionate presentations usually ended with a standing ovation.

It had taken years and losing everything for Keith to become whole again. In his new line of work, he was making a difference for the industry and people he cared about. Eventually, he established a charity in Ginny Bronson's memory. The ashes of his past had become his crowning purpose.

## C.O.D.E. Conduct

### Profiling Keith's Reactions

PTSD can come on gradually, accumulating from a multiplicity of stressful events. Or as in Keith's case, it can be triggered by one dramatic incident. Post-Traumatic Stress Disorder, in its simplest definition, is a normal response to abnormal stress. Some people are able to find healthy coping methods through self-care practices, but most benefit from the guidance of a professional.

If you are experiencing any of the signs or symptoms listed on the sites below, we recommend you consult with a professional for an initial evaluation.

## Questions to Consider

- **How might Keith have dealt with the trauma beginning on his first day in a healthier way?**
- **Could Keith's marriage have been saved? If so, how?**
- **Why do you think prescription pain killers are a common go-to for those in emotional distress?**

## C.O.D.E. Conduct

**Communication** — When you are acting out in ways that even confuse you, ask yourself what is really going on. You can't identify the causes of your behavior if you don't identify the origin of your wounds. Speak honestly with at least one safe person about the things you are struggling with.

**Objectiveness** — Do an internal assessment of your life's biggest events. Draw a timeline, marking traumas and celebrations, then ask yourself how those moments influenced your life today.

**Dedication** — Don't allow past trauma to undermine your most important relationships. Dedicate yourself to doing everything within your power to fight in a healthy way for the people you care about most.

**Engagement** — What happened yesterday is not taking place in the present moment. Too often, we get stuck, reliving a past disaster or painful event. Don't ignore the opportunities, hope, and joys in front of you now.

# Firefighter Summary

Most people recognize the heroic efforts of firefighters, who are essential to public safety, but they are often unfamiliar with the under-publicized consequences of their job. Not only do they put out fires, but they rescue people from burning cars, buildings and other dangerous situations. They commonly save animals as well as human life, but not without significant risk to their bodies and social relationships.

Also, there are other more subtle perils firefighters must contend with. According to reports published in *Science Daily*, the frequent exposure to carcinogenic chemicals, inhaled and absorbed through the skin, increases their chances of contracting some forms of cancer.

Because of their consistent interactions with flames and smoke, firefighters are also threatened with burns of varying degrees — minor blisters, third degree, and even fatal flames are prospects. Firefighters must often enter burning buildings where weakened roofs, floors, stairwells, and doors can collapse on them without warning. Muscle strains and bone breaks are common occurrences due to the heights they must climb and the gear they must wear.

Twenty-four hour shifts for days at a time can place vice-grip pressures on a marriage, quality time with children, and extended family relationships. The firefighting life may look glamorous on the outside, but insiders know the secret perils at work. Yet, nothing compares to the sooty smile of a child when placed in the hands of their parent, or a hug from an elderly person whose home was just saved. These are the rewards for valiance.

This section is dedicated to the men and women who douse the blazes that jeopardize human safety. You are highly regarded, and we appreciate your courage.

## Chapter 13
## Smoke and Burn

The alarm clanged in rapid succession. The sounds of running feet echoed in harmony with the bell as Roger joined the five men and two women from House 4 in the race to contain the flames that rousted them from their sleep. Roger hurried into his gear, slapping his fire helmet on last, as he swung himself onto engine 23. The door raised and they were off in less than two minutes. He looked at his watch — 0224.

A small flame lapped the wooden window shutters on the right side of the one floor boxed residence as the firetruck screeched to a stop. The exterior siding appeared pale gray through the shadowed haze of night. As the crew bolted from the engine, a man's silhouette smothered the tiny fire at the door with something that looked like a blanket.

All movement stopped in unison at the sound of the silhouette's demands. A man's voice echoed across the night air. "Stop where you are. I have a gun."

Roger froze where he stood.

Several long seconds passed, then the chief's calm, controlled response broke the silence. "Please don't shoot, sir. We're here to help, not hurt you. We just need to fight this fire."

The chief whispered discreetly, "Roger, can you get to the engine and call this in to Cen-Com?"

"Yes, sir." Roger slowly and silently backed up, afraid to take his eyes off of the shadowed form standing in the doorway.

The man shouted again. "You get out of here. You hear me now. Get out!"

The chief answered, "What about the fire? We need to put it out."

"It's already out."

"But it can smolder unseen and reignite before you

realize it."

"I said it's out." The click of a firearm's hammer was unmistakable.

The shadows of the chief's hand motions told everyone to ease their way back to the engine. "Okay, sir. We aren't here to upset you. Let us load up, and we'll leave you alone."

"The quicker the better."

"That's our plan."

Roger flinched, slowly releasing the button on the radio. Cen-Com had informed him that law enforcement was already en route, with an ETA of one minute. A neighbor had called in to report the shouting match between the homeowner and the chief.

As the sound of police sirens grew close, the man yelled, "I'm not lettin' no cops in my house. This is private property."

Maintaining his composure, the chief replied, "That'll be between you and them, sir. We're only here for the fire." The chief inched backwards and whispered over his shoulder, "Is everyone in the clear?"

"Yes, sir," Roger, who had reached the chief, whispered back.

Suddenly, three cars flashing blue and red pulled into the driveway. A shot rang through the ebony air, but most didn't hear it, the sound was swallowed by siren wails.

Roger, like everyone else on the scene, was distracted by the dramatic arrival. But the second gunshot wasn't muffled by sirens, and it caused Roger to instinctively drop behind the firetruck.

The officers spilled from their vehicles and strategically took cover. The officer in charge shouted at Roger and the rest of the fire crew, "Get down!" It was an unnecessary command, but nonetheless appreciated.

In a matter of seconds, Roger and the rest of the House 4 crew were securely huddled behind their fire engine, witnesses to the verbal debate between the male voice guarding the house and the police captain, attempting to reason with him. Thirty-five minutes later, it became obvious all efforts were in vain.

A loud crack split the silence of the night, sounding like another gunshot, almost at the precise moment a new flame blazed hot enough to burst through a window a couple of feet to the left of where the man had stood. Only now, his shadowed frame was missing. He lay crumpled in the doorway.

At the wave of the police captain's hands, a few officers crept forward, splitting into groups on two sides. When they neared the doorway, the officers entered in force.

They surrounded the perpetrator and pointed their guns inside the residence. Even in the darkness, you could see the change in their body language — from tensed to relaxed. A voice shouted, "All clear, Cap. He's dead. Self-inflicted. But looks like he started another fire before he pulled the trigger, it's burning good and picking up speed."

The police captain raised from behind his defensive cover, then turned and addressed the fire chief, "Can you douse the fire, but try to preserve as much evidence as possible? I'd like to leave the perp's body where it is until the coroner can get in, unless you think we have to move it sooner."

"We'll do what we can." The chief stood and spoke to Roger, "You heard the captain, gather your team, and let's get to work."

Carefully, they worked the scene. Roger's crew carried the fire hose toward the broken window and began to spray into the house with full pressure. It didn't take long for them to contain the fire, allowing them to don their breathing masks and make entry.

Roger's flashlight cut through the smoky haze, allowing him to see a foot in front of him. By the looks of the scorched couch and recliner, he guessed he was in the living room. As Roger shuffled cautiously, he noted that most of the room appeared to be gutted and fire had spread to the kitchen.

One of his team members, Jerry, called out. "Beds are burned in two rooms down the hall, but he only let it get the beds."

Roger was perplexed. He noted the oddity of small fires burning in different locations. He wondered, *Why would anyone burn beds and couches inside their home and then put them out?* A sick feeling started in his gut, as he recalled the man's demeanor when they arrived.

After a cursory look throughout the building to ensure all embers were out, Roger circled back and inched his way to the living room again. This time, he approached the couch for a closer look. Through the springs, his flashlight illuminated something curious. On closer inspection, Roger confirmed what he feared — human bones. They were laying next to the charred remains of a mid-sized canine.

Jerry shouted from the hall, "Roger, we're gonna need law enforcement in here. I've got human remains. Small ones."

With dejection tainting his voice, Roger answered, "Me too. Check the other bedroom."

A minute later, the sadness in Jerry's answer confirmed what Roger didn't want to hear. "Even smaller ones. Toddler size."

Roger inhaled oxygen from his mask before speaking again, then he said, "Let's move out so we don't contaminate the scene any more. We've done all we can." He glanced down at the corpse of the man with the gun on his way out, wondering how anyone could kill a child before taking their own life — then for a moment, Roger's own impending divorce crossed his mind.

Some of the insane thoughts he'd had suddenly reinserted themselves from memory — and he looked down again. Maybe the man was more human than monster, giving way to the desperation that sometimes teased Roger. He shuddered as he crossed the yard back to the truck.

The fire department stayed on scene as a precaution, should another flame sprout from the ashes. Every fire fighter felt the weight of the discoveries made by Roger and Jerry. The night lingered long for each of them.

When daybreak washed the horizon with its orange, red, and yellow hues, darkness remained in Roger's soul. It deepened after Roger conferred with the coroner and police captain before they extricated all of the remains. The coroner confirmed two adults and three children were in the house.

The other adult body was found huddled in a corner of the bathtub, burned, though not completely. The police captain said they found gun casings near all of the bodies, leading to the assumption that all were dead before the fires were started. Roger hoped that meant they died quickly.

For those watching the careful removal of the bagged remains from the residence, a somber reverence held them temporarily frozen in place. But as the last bag was being lifted into the coroner's car, the sound of a vehicle crunching loose rocks on the driveway broke the solemnity of the moment.

Apparently, the first family members had gotten word. The last sound Roger heard as their fire engine pulled away, was the haunting echo of a woman's mournful screams. They would torment his dreams and impact his decisions for weeks to come — leading to major changes at work and at home.

Roger changed his perspective about his divorce. He determined not to let the mental demons have their way. So instead of sparring with his ex-wife, he began to work with her, reminding himself repeatedly that what their children needed most was parents who behaved maturely. It surprised him to find the less he fought for what he'd thought were his rights, the less she did. Arguments were prevented before they started, reminding Roger of the Proverb, *A gentle answer turns away anger.*

They were soon able to reach an amicable agreement, their kids were happier, and Roger's work performance improved. His inner fire had been put out, too.

### Profiling Roger's Reactions

Most conflicts, especially domestic, are grounded in right-fighting. A demand that others give us our way, fueled by fear that we might lose something important. But if the battle rages on for too long or we dig our heels in too deeply, escalated emotions can reach a danger zone.

In many murder/suicides, the full truth is rarely learned

about why they commit heinous acts, especially when children are involved. Roger was wise to learn from someone else's mistake, refusing to allow pride and a stubborn heart to lead him to costly decisions. Unhealthy thoughts and emotions can do strange things to our minds and propel us to act in ways we would otherwise never consider, under normal conditions.

## Questions to Consider

- **What imaginations likely played on Roger about his impending divorce?**
- **How can a normal, balanced person, transform into someone who harms themselves and others?**
- **What difference would it make if people didn't speak and shout from their anger during conflict?**

## C.O.D.E. Conduct

**Communication** — Call your spouse or another family member and simply say, "I appreciate you." Most people hunger for simple recognition, and there's nothing like experiencing a near loss to remind you to take positive actions with the people around you — even those you are estranged from.

**Objectiveness** — Most of what we fear never happens. Don't dwell on the what-ifs, focus on the facts — especially when your emotions escalate after being exposed to a traumatic scene. Emotions themselves are not bad, they can actually be a catalyst for great good. What we do with them will bring about consequences, either negative or positive, depending on how we respond.

**Dedication** — Set your mind to being a teachable, coachable, and trainable person. Don't allow stubbornness to steal your potential for strong relationships, lucrative promotions, and a happier life. If you're open to it, even bad situations can lead to greater good. Terrible things happen between people every day, and if you work in any area of emergency services, you will likely see the worst of them. But the question is, "How can you make something positive out of the bitter things you are exposed to?"

**Engagement** — Seeing a child injured or worse, can drain the hope from your soul. But hanging out with children and laughing with them provides powerful healing. If you have kids of your own, schedule time each week doing something fun with them. If you have nieces or nephews, find out what they enjoy and arrange to engage with them. Or take a foster, orphaned, or child of divorce for a recreational excursion. Sadly, too many children today do not have access to safe adults who will engage with them in healthy activities. Do for one child what you wish you could do for all children.

# Chapter 14
# Drowning in Adrenalin

Carole Garber glanced at the time while she looked at her weather app — then she groaned. It was 3:45 a.m. Wednesday. And from the sound of the rain torrent pounding Carole's roof, Hurricane Harvey was staying true to the devastating reputation that proceeded it.

According to her app, over fifteen inches of rain had fallen in Carole's Beaumont neighborhood in less than eight hours. By the time the deluge ended, that number would exceed 51 inches — crushing the lower 48 states record for amount of rain ever recorded from a tropical system — 26 inches fell in 24 hours alone. The alert that had woken Carole, held the promise her team was going to put in some crazy hours. The signs were not pointing to a good outcome for the Lone Star State. Carole was being called and she had forty-five minutes to report.

Carole stumbled to the kitchen after a pit stop to pick up her TV remote. She hit the button on her coffee pot, then pushed the red power button on the remote. Kevin Roth, a senior meteorologist for The Weather Channel was talking. He said, "The Beaumont/Port Arthur area has gotten about half a year's worth of rain in one day."

Addicks and Barker Reservoirs confluenced with the Buffalo Bayou watershed, causing an unprecedented amount of water pouring into Beaumont and Port Arthur's streets, cars, and homes.

The first bloated body Carole and her teammates had to pull from the murky mess was that of an elderly man. He slipped from Carole's grasp on her first try, forcing her to reach back into the putrid soup to clutch his shirt collar and jean waistband.

A few feet away, a small blonde head bobbed with the undulation of the fire and rescue boat's waves. He was a sickeningly light lift — the little guy looked to be between two and three-years-old. If Carole had a son, she imagined he might look like the deceased boy she now held in her arms. She shoved the emotions inching up her throat and back down into the pit of her gut. . .where they belonged.

For thirty-nine straight hours, Carole and her fellow firefighters waded through water saturated with filth, while they piled dead bodies and living people into their boats. They covered the shoulders of the living with light blankets, even though the humidity was suffocating and the temps blazing hot. The other blankets were draped over the faces of the dead, laid respectfully across the bottom of the boat. Some lifted prayers to their God in Heaven, while others relied on motivating self-talk to get them through the aftermath of nature gone wild. All were focused on the crisis at hand.

Back and forth they traveled, loading and unloading people and bodies from buildings and water onto dry land. They expended themselves until the very last drop of adrenalin was gone. In the thirty-sixth hour, Carole hit the brick wall of physical fatigue, emotional paralysis, and mental meltdown. But she pushed through for another rescue attempt. *Maybe we can save one more*, she thought. They pulled a teen girl from a balcony window.

Carole got a small boost of renewed energy. *Just one more*. This time, they were able to get a family of three into the boat. As soon as they unloaded them, Bob, a firefighter from Carole's station, said, "My arms are gelatin, I need twenty."

"No shame in taking care of yourself so you can care for others," the chief said. "Carole, do you need a breather?"

"I'm good for another run," Carole said, fighting the reality of her condition.

"All right," the chief gunned the boat motor, and they sped toward their next pickup. It took less than four minutes to find it.

The water was receding. It had given the driver of a white SUV the illusion that he could cross a low area of the highway, topping the channel of the seriously swollen river. He didn't make it.

The nose of the SUV pointed downward and danced as the wheels on the back end bounced off of the broken pavement. It appeared as if it was hung up on something, preventing full submersion.

Like a pointer hunting dog, the chief's eyes locked on the vehicle. He spoke out loud, but Carole wasn't sure he was talking to her, or to himself.

"Flooded streams often camouflage pockets of abyss, making it appear as if there's a solid roadway when the asphalt has washed away, leaving a deep ravine for unsuspecting people to drive into. Debris, tangles of wire and wood, even large appliances are often hidden beneath a chocolatey surface. You can't see swirling eddies until you are on top of them."

A loud crack thundered as the large piece of highway where the SUV's back tires were lodged broke away.

Water pushed out from the impact site, causing a small tsunami to race toward their rescue boat. The chief acted instantly, moving them away from the dangerous tide and closer to the bobbing vehicle. The driver would only be able to survive for a couple of minutes or maybe just seconds.

As the chief navigated them closer, the head of a dark-haired man popped out of the driver's side window. He scrambled out of the window and scaled to a squatted position on top, screaming, "Help," the entire time.

The chief returned to narrative mode. "That SUV's at risk for somersaulting. We've got to get him off there, quick."

"Carole, the waters moving too swiftly, and there's too much debris for me to take my hand off the motor's throttle and my eyes off of the river. Can you toss him the line and pull him in by yourself?"

Her first instinct was to tell the truth — but instead, she lied. "I can do it, Chief."

"We don't have any time to waste. Throw the rope."

The first time Carole threw it, she was way off. The lasso landed a good four feet in front of the vehicle.

"Try again. There's no time to waste on frustration," the chief yelled.

Her second toss hit the guy's hand, but slipped through as if it were coated with melted butter.

"Again," the chief encouraged.

Carole's arms burned from the inside out. Every fiber in her muscles wanted to lock up. *Not now,* she willed. *You CAN do this,* she demanded of her body. The toss was off again, but closer than the first time.

"Again."

Carole wanted to tell him to get off her back, but instead, said to herself, *Focus. Keep your eyes on your target all the way through the throw. Don't give up.* This time everything came together. Carole hurled and hit the mark perfectly. The man clutched it and was not letting go. Now for the hard part. Carole had to hoist him into their boat.

The chief hollered above the roar of the rolling river. "You're going to have to jump in. When you do, kick and swim toward us with everything you have. We'll pull on this end. When I count, you jump on three." In a lower voice, he said to Carole. "I'm going to try to help you, but I will literally have seconds before my hands have to be back on this motor — or we're all going down. Understand?"

"Yes, sir." Carole tried to shield the expression of the fear she felt.

The chief yelled out, "Here we go. Are you ready?"

"Yes," the man said.

"All right. One. Two. Three!"

The man splashed into the murky mess, then kicked and stroked feverishly.

Carole groaned as she pulled. She could feel the body heat from the chief, as tugged with her.

It felt like everything moved in slow motion. The man was making his way toward them, but by inches, not by feet.

"Pull harder," the chief screamed in Carole's ear.

Adrenalin surged her veins again. She wasn't sure where this dose came from, since she had long ago depleted all her reserves. But the energy did its work. The man seemed to show up at the edge of their boat, without Carole seeing him span the necessary distance.

The moment gravity tipped his body more inside the boat than out, the chief dropped the rope and regained control of the motor. The man flopped into the bottom of the boat like a fish.

Relief flooded Carole's body and soul. By the time they delivered their patient safely to the drop off point, Carole was spent. Her legs could barely hold her up to walk. She collapsed after just six steps.

Sirens were blaring when Carole became coherent a few minutes later. She tried to push the oxygen mask off her face to tell them she was okay, but a strong hand stilled her efforts and forced it securely into place. She closed her eyes, far too tired to resist.

The hospital kept Carole overnight for observation, and

she was released the next morning. The chief came to see her while she was signing her discharge papers. "I want you to take a few days off."

"But there are so many people who still need help. You need me."

"You'd be amazed at how far the water has receded since yesterday. We've got lots of fresh volunteers showing up to assist, and we've already saved hundreds of people. We won't need as much manpower now. So what I really need from you is for you to fully recuperate. It's going to take our city a long time to recover from this."

"But. . . ."

"There will be no more discussion. My decision is made. If you show up at the station before Saturday, I'll write you up. Understand?"

It was Tuesday.

Carole lowered her head. "Yes, Chief."

*Maybe I can get a few things done around the house,* she thought. Little did she know.

When she got home, Carole was surprised at how exhausted she actually felt — mentally and emotionally, as well as physically. Try as she might, she could not motivate herself to get up off the couch, much less to do anything productive. When her best friend showed up with homemade chicken soup and a bag of nutritious groceries, she didn't react as she normally would have, with ongoing objections. Instead, she offered a weak, "Thanks."

Her friend didn't stay long.

Carole slept the majority of her three days off, drifting in and out. She'd never felt so wiped in all her life. She felt better by Saturday when she returned to work, but not really refreshed. It would take nearly six months before that happened.

## Profiling Carole's Reactions

When you've come through any kind of traumatic event, you often expect your body and spirit to rebound much more quickly than they are capable of. Emergencies are not just hard on the souls of victims, but those who save and treat them are often impacted long-term as well. Carole had an unreasonable expectation for her own recovery — she downplayed her experience in hopes it would go away on its own — something that does not happen.

### Questions to Consider

- **How do weather events and other unknown elements add fear to a disastrous situation?**
- **When in the midst of a trauma, how can human emotions make things worse? Is there a way to prepare for and prevent emotional problems from happening?**
- **What kind of resources are available to help emergency service workers deal with the echoing effects of what they've seen?**

## C.O.D.E. Conduct

**Communication** — Pride and fear are hazardous voices to listen to. You can put the lives of others in danger if you attempt to push past your physical and mental limits, versus heeding the inner warning signs that tell you to catch your breath. Especially in the midst of an ongoing traumatic event, you will need periodic breaks, brief yes, but also necessary. So speak up, breathe, then get right back to it.

**Objectiveness** — A desire to help others is the main motive for most who enter emergency services. But don't allow your emotional drive to save or assist someone put you in a position that harms instead of helps. If you push beyond your strength and become too weak to serve, your body could give out at the worst possible time.

**Dedication** — Commit to being honest with yourself and others. Dedication to the job means doing it at your optimal ability.

**Engagement** — When you are in a position where you have no choice but to push beyond your limits, don't beat yourself up. Do your best and rest when you can. Then when family and friends offer support, accept it.

# Chapter 15
# Recovery Mission

Derek Bando had worked for the Lansbury Elite Search and Rescue Team for just under two years. He and his partner, Brett Rawlings, were trained to rappel into tight, cramped caves, mine shafts, and sink holes, as well as to look for victims in fire and and water emergencies. They were both highly experienced in crawling inside tight spaces while using sophisticated breathing equipment, although Brett had a couple of years on Derek. But nothing in their backgrounds prepared them for Ellie Macon.

The call came in on a Sunday. Derek had just returned home from church with his family. Brett was preparing to barbecue.

Several months prior, a young nineteen-year-old woman was reported missing. Investigators were convinced her husband had killed her — with a girlfriend on the side as his motive.

To hear hubby tell it, they had gotten into an argument while hiking in the high desert at the outskirts of the city, and as soon as they returned home, Ellie had packed up and left him. She was never heard from or seen again. Ellie hadn't even texted or called her mother, something she regularly did every day.

But the investigators had gotten a break in the case.

A friend of the husband had come forward with a phone he'd found in a duffle bag the husband had left at his house the day following Ellie's disappearance. The friend had forgotten about the bag until he stumbled across it in his tool shed. For investigators, the telephone provided a gold mine of evidence.

The phone held incriminating texts between the husband and girlfriend on the day Ellie went missing, but there were pictures the husband had taken on the hike. The team felt certain the images were trophies, documenting the exact area he'd dumped Ellie's body. The area was known for its multiplicity of small shafts and caves.

Two weeks into the initial search, the investigators located her body. They needed Derek and Brett's expertise to retrieve it from the deep crevice.

In a local television interview about the high profile case, Derek later said, "I had no idea what we were getting into."

Brett added, "I was told they found a body, approximately 140 feet in a mine shaft, but in a situation like that, you never know what you're actually dealing with until you drop down."

"Do you ever feel scared or claustrophobic?" the interviewer probed.

Derek said, "When we arrived on scene, they told us they had detected propane gas fumes. The description of the whole scenario sounded pretty precarious to me. And to make it more difficult, the soil type we were facing wasn't really that stable, making the deep environment more dangerous. The entrance was questionable for us. So I don't know if I'd say I was scared, but I definitely used extra caution."

Brett added, "We're used to risking our lives to save people, but I have to admit, this situation sounded especially perilous. And I'm claustrophobic anyway. I had second thoughts about endangering my own life to pull out someone who had already lost theirs. Leaving my wife and kids alone for a dead body just didn't appeal to me."

Derek jumped in again, "It's risk versus gain. Do I want to do this? No. But can I turn my back on the situation? No. We knew if we could pull Ellie's body out of that shaft, it could help investigators solve her murder. So, in spite of our reservations, we agreed to do it."

Brett said, "I drew the short straw and descended first." He shifted uneasily in his chair as his eyes took on the glaze of memories relived. "When they lowered me into the pit, I eventually reached a point much deeper than I'd ever been. Rocks slid along the sides. I knew what a sudden collapse could mean for me — the end." He ran his finger across his neck for effect.

Derek chuckled nervously.

Brett continued, "I couldn't help noticing a few snakes, they were obviously offended by the light beam on my helmet. They moved into defensive mode as I passed them on my way down. I kept cringing, waiting for the strike." Sweat beaded on Brett's upper lip, as if on cue. "And the heat was obnoxious. Below the earth's surface, it had to be 90 degrees, because the temperature topside was 110 degrees just before I was harnessed in. I had to talk myself past claustrophobia with every inch my hoist took me deeper into that black hole. It's something you simply can't describe."

Derek nodded agreement.

Brett continued, "Under those conditions, you only have a limited amount of effectiveness before the heat, the weight of your equipment, and your emotions fatigue you beyond your ability to perform. I was almost spent as I neared the floor of the shaft, but I caught sight of something that pumped adrenalin and gave me a second wind."

Brett's chin quivered, every so slightly. "I could tell it was a leg — a human leg. And by the woman's purple tennis shoe, I knew we had found Ellie."

The interviewer let out a disturbing gasp. "What was going through your mind in that moment?"

Brett said, "We see a lot of death in this line of work, and you develop a method of blocking out your emotions for a little while. The job you have to do helps. It allows you to focus until you're away from the situation. Later, the emotions hit. It's not like you can escape your feelings, but you can avoid them when you need to. You kind of get used to it, except you really don't."

Derek's responsive expression said he felt the same way.

"The original plan was for me to complete the operation, extracting Ellie from her desert tomb. But after being down almost an hour, my body was fatigued and I could feel myself dehydrating. So when I didn't respond, my captain opted to pull me up and send Derek in."

Brett's brown eyes were now highlighted with a distinct glaze. "When I finally got out of the mine, I took my mask off. I didn't realize yet what it had protected my senses from. The stench I had been immersed in and didn't smell while I was in the shaft had saturated my clothes, and now burned me with its odor. I started dry heaving. But in all honesty, I was vomiting as much over the emotional junk I'd stuffed, as the smell itself."

Derek picked up the conversation with his part of the story. "My assignment? Get the body in a bag so it could be retrieved. I was not excited. I'd never put a body in a bag. Plus, I was scared that rocks would fall, knocking out the shaft floor beneath Ellie. I didn't know how much further she might drop, or if we would ever be able to recover her if that happened."

Brett confessed, "I never told you before, but I was worried about the same thing. We were very close to getting her out. But all it would have taken was a single slip, and she would have been gone forever. And all of the evidence would have disappeared with her. Ellie wasn't the only thing at the bottom of the pit. There was a bottle with liquid and a rag stuffed inside, near her head. A barbecue lighter was lying near her feet. It looked like someone tried to set her on fire after they threw her in. Thankfully, they weren't successful."

Derek nodded. "Finally, I was able to put her into the bag without loosening the ground below. I gathered the obvious evidence and secured it in a smaller bag, before they hoisted me up. When they pulled me back up to the sand, and I looked over at the black plastic outline of her body, I lost it. I retreated behind one of the emergency vehicles to compose myself before anyone noticed. I actually wept."

He touched his right eye with his index finger. "I've viewed dozens of dead bodies, but maybe it was having to bag her that did it. Or perhaps the way that precious young lady was tossed like garbage into that vile pit. I did calm down and managed to hold it together. . .until I got home. Then I fell apart. I'm still not sure I've fully recovered from that day."

The interview ended with both men lowering their heads to hide the emotions overtaking them.

It took three years for Ellie's case to go to trial. Her husband was sentenced to life plus twenty. Derek and Brett were sentenced to exposure sensitivity, where anything activating their memories of this case caused them to struggle with old memories and pent-up emotions. Both men were able to move on, but Ellie's ghost followed them — she was someone they would never forget.

### Profiling Derek's Reactions

No one ever really gets used to dealing with the dead — no matter what they tell themselves. Those who do it daily develop a calloused normalcy as they go about the business of retrieving, processing, and studying human remains — or at least they appear to.

For some, the job does not always mean direct contact with dead bodies, so when it happens, it can stir emotions. In Derek's experience, the case was dramatically infused with the passions of community members, media, and other emergency services people, so emotions ran especially high. The swirl of factors created a perfect storm, magnifying feelings of horror for all involved.

### Questions to Consider

- **Have you ever had to put your job ahead of your family or risked your life in the line of duty?**
- **Do you think Derek's emotional state after the mission was warranted? Why or why not?**
- **How does media coverage impact emotions in highly publicized cases?**

### C.O.D.E. Conduct

**Communication** — Even when you can't share all the details of a mission, you still need to communicate (with a safe person) how it has left you mentally. Talking through your thoughts and emotions can prevent negative strongholds taking control. Whatever you bring into the light will dissipate: pessimism, fear, and other haunting memories, can only flourish in the darkness of secrecy.

**Objectiveness** — Reminding yourself of the mission, and why the risk is important can help you maintain your focus when your thoughts threaten to undermine your effectiveness. When you are thrust into a situation where you are forced to deal with strained emotions, concentrate on why what you are doing is so crucial.

**Dedication** — Because of your chosen profession, it will at times, become necessary to risk your life or the well-being of your family. Even mundane work schedules can cause you to miss out on family events, birthdays, and special holiday gatherings. However, just because you can't establish *normal* timelines doesn't mean you can't celebrate. Schedule something special with your family and friends as soon as possible following events you are forced to miss.

**Engagement** — Sometimes the quickest road to recovery comes from connecting with a person or project close to a case victim. Helping others heal often provides a healthy dose of mental medicine.

# Chapter 16
# Final Abuse

Their ladder truck parked next to the red and blue lights of several police cars. Dispatch had called out an ambulance, but it hadn't arrived on scene yet.

Janet Blanton rolled out with the rest of her crew, medic bag in hand.

Officer Ryan Villa stepped out of his patrol car and walked into the impromptu huddle of firefighters. "Call came in from an elderly woman, but I'm not sure what we're really dealing with here."

"What's the story?" a voice from the fire group said.

"She said her husband was bleeding, but claims she has no idea what happened. The woman told 9-1-1 that a stranger must have broken in after she went to bed. Said she got up to go to the bathroom and saw him laying by his bed on the floor. Bleeding."

"Wasn't she in bed with him?" Janet said.

"No idea. I guess they sleep in separate bedrooms. My grandparents do." Villa said.

A radio crackled. "Scene's cleared for entry."

Janet moved toward the door at her captain's command.

The house looked normal. Neat, orderly, tidy — everything in its place.

A female officer waved Janet over to a recliner enveloping a frail-looking, silver-haired woman. Her right hand appeared to be bleeding, and the front of her shirt was covered in crimson splatters. Her right temple was smudged with blood, and it stained her white strands of loose hair, likely when she pushed it out of her eyes.

Janet knelt down in front of the chair. "Ma'am, are you okay?"

"Yes," her voice croaked. "Somebody came in and hurt Jim. Why would they hurt Jim?"

"I don't know, but the police will do a thorough investigation," Janet patted the woman's hand. *She must be in shock. Poor thing can't even cry.*

Janet put the pressure cuff around the woman's tiny wrist and pumped. "What's your name?"

"Donna. Donna Franklin. We just celebrated our forty-fourth anniversary. Our son and two daughters came in from out of town. We even had all our grandkids here."

"It sounds nice," Janet said.

The woman's face took on a faraway look. "It was one of the best days we've had in years. I almost forgot. . ."

Janet waited for the woman to answer but after several seconds, she had to ask the question. "Almost forgot what?"

The older woman lowered her eyes. "It doesn't matter anymore. It's all over now."

"What's over?"

"I can't talk about it. We don't even discuss it with each other. Secrets and lies. Our marriage has been nothing but secrets and lies."

Officer Villa, whose job was to keep watch, had been standing near the kitchen doorway. He edged closer as the woman talked to Janet. He rolled his finger at Janet, in a keep-going motion.

"Donna, what secrets and lies?"

"Jim's secrets and lies. Forty-four years of secrets and lies."

Janet reached out and held the woman's trembling hands. "What did he do to you, Donna?"

"I found it by accident. I don't get on the computer much, not as much as Jim did. Our granddaughter taught us how to use it. I wanted to look up a new chicken recipe. I get bored sometimes and like to try different things for dinner. He forgot to close the computer down, like Abby taught us. So when I moved the mouse, it came up. I felt so sick when I saw it."

Detective Warren had joined Officer Villa, and both were standing directly behind the recliner. Officer Villa again motioned with his finger for Janet to continue.

Janet squeezed the woman's fingers gently, "What did you see?"

"His email was open. I saw her name, and what he was writing to her. He signed our grandson's name. Our grandson. He's twenty." The woman looked down at her lap. "And what Jim said to that girl was wrong. It took my breath away."

Though she had no idea where the woman's story was going, Janet swallowed hard, to keep her emotions from taking over.

A single tear slipped off the woman's high cheekbone. "I typed in the girl's name to search for other emails, and several came up. They had been in contact for months. He was planning to meet her. In Georgia." The woman looked up and locked angry eyes with Janet. "What was he going to tell that girl when she saw him? He's an old man. She thought he was twenty years old. He even sent pictures of our grandson, Chad. How could he pretend to be our grandson? It's so twisted and sick."

Janet felt nauseous. She'd never heard anything so vile and offensive.

"He got prostate cancer. A few months ago. Stage four. Terminal. He was going through chemo and radiation. He couldn't take me anywhere, we couldn't do anything, he couldn't help me around the house anymore. I handled all of that just fine, but not this. Do you know what it's like to find out I've been married to a pervert all these years? I wasted my whole life on him. What if my kids and grandkids found out?" The woman looked at her hands as she played her fingers nervously. Then she glanced at Janet. "Was I supposed to just take it? Was I supposed to take care of him after I knew he was a pervert? I knew he was going to die eventually, but how long did I have to wait?"

Janet shifted her weight. What she was hearing was becoming more and more uncomfortable.

"I wanted to be done with it. Done with him. I felt like I was in prison, between the care-taking and his messes. I didn't want to clean up his puke and poop anymore. My oldest daughter drove him to his last treatment and oncologist visit. She said they were told he was doing better than they expected. That he could actually survive. I know it makes me a monster, but I didn't want him to live. He controlled me our whole marriage. He acted nice in front of other people, but he never let me do anything I wanted to. He yelled at me and called me names when no one else was around. The kids have heard it, but they covered for him like I did."

A waterfall of tears poured off her face as she continued.

"I wanted it all to end. I gave him my most productive and energetic years. I put up with his verbal and emotional abuse, and this is how he paid me back? By chasing a girl young enough to be his granddaughter? What kind of man does that? What kind of woman puts up with it? So I ended it. All of it. I ended him."

Janet pulled back slightly, but the woman continued talking, unable to stop.

"Some of his meds make him sleepy. So tonight, I gave him a little extra, just to make sure. Then I got my big butcher knife and walked into his room. We quit sharing a bed a long time ago, because of my snoring. I called his name softly. But he didn't answer, so I knew it was safe. I crept up to his bed and looked down on him. He was sleeping so peacefully, and that just made me madder. How dare he sleep well? He made the mess, not me. Why did I have to be the one to clean it up? Why was I the one upset? It should have been him. I stabbed him in the chest the first time. It felt really strange, but in a good way. His eyes opened up real wide, and he looked straight at me. That scared me. So I pulled the knife out fast, before he had a chance to grab me, and I stabbed him again. In the leg. I thought it would stop him from getting up and chasing me if I ran. But he didn't get up. He just laid there and looked at me. He didn't say a word. I wanted him to stop looking at me. So I pulled the knife out of his leg, and I stabbed him in the belly. That one made him curl up, and when he did, he rolled out of the bed onto the floor. I think he's still there."

Janet rocked back on her knees and just stared at the woman.. *How could this sweet little lady have done something so brutal? But then how could her husband have acted so evil and perverted? What kind of world are we living in?* Something inside Janet clicked.

After three infant deaths in the past week and an apartment fire collapse last week that took the life of their junior captain and eleven civilians, this senseless situation was the Jenga® piece that caused her internal tower of justice to fall. *It's all unfair,* Janet thought. Immediately followed by, *You don't have time for this. Pull yourself together and do your job.*

Janet willed herself back into action.

After cleaning, medicating, and wrapping the woman's sliced finger, checking her vitals, and finding nothing else wrong, Janet gently pushed stained, unruly strands of hair out of the woman's face. Then she nodded to Detective Warren, who waited patiently behind the chair.

The detective walked around in silence. "Mrs. Franklin, I'm sorry to have to tell you this, but you are under arrest. I need to cuff you and read you your Miranda rights. Do you understand?"

Janet felt a strange detachment to what she was seeing and hearing. *I should be appalled right now. I should object to them cuffing a little old lady.* But Janet remained posed. Instead, she watched as the officers carefully clicked the handcuffs onto the woman's tiny wrists and tenderly guided Mrs. Franklin toward the door. Numbness was the only thing Janet felt.

The triggering effects of the elder murder did not dissipate in a matter of days, as Janet hoped. She found it increasingly difficult to connect emotionally to the crises, concerns, and compassions of others, including her own family. She began forgetting important dates, such as birthdays and anniversaries. When it happened with her own children, Janet got scared. *Am I losing my mind? I always do something special to celebrate my kids' birthdays. What is going on with me?*

After a while, Janet simply learned to live with the frostier version of herself. She didn't like the woman in the mirror, but she soon grew awkwardly comfortable with her new persona. It was easier to keep the barrier up.

Four years later, Janet's fire house, along with others in the city, combined funds to bring in a speaker who addressed Secondary Traumatic Stress, or Compassion Fatigue. Janet didn't know what it was, but she was intrigued by what she heard. The subject hit close to home.

After the session, Janet waited until the long line of enthusiastic firefighters trickled through, then confided to the speaker, "I can't remember important dates related to my family and friends any more. I'm letting a lot of things fall through the cracks. Detail used to be my forte, but I can't remember details to save my soul now. I'm frustrated with myself, but I can't seem to feel much for anyone else. However, I can drive by a scene I've worked and recall every vivid detail about what happened. What is wrong with me?"

The woman placed a soothing hand on Janet's shoulder. "There's nothing wrong with you. I'm not a psychologist, certified counselor, or therapist, so I can't diagnose you. However, working with people in your field, I've met others who've described the things you just did. They were eventually diagnosed with Secondary Traumatic Stress."

The speaker bent down and lifted a pamphlet from her merchandise table. "There are online resources where you can take assessments, learn some self-care techniques, and will prove you are not alone in what you are facing. You can find the information here." She handed Janet the brochure. "But I strongly urge you to seek professional counseling with someone who can accurately determine where you are and what you need to find some answers."

Janet wished she could cry, but her tears had long ago dried up. She did, however, feel the first hint of hope she'd had in a very long time.

Within forty-five days, Janet was surprised at how much better she felt — relieved, at peace, and free. She had tried one counselor, but it soon became apparent he was not the right fit. She felt an immediate connection with the second therapist though. Janet quickly found the woman a safe place to vent, and within two sessions, she was telling her things she'd never spoken out loud to another person. It was terrifying the first time, but Janet now knew it was exhilarating to pop the cork on her bottled-up emotions.

Janet was diagnosed with Compassion Fatigue, otherwise known as Secondary Traumatic Stress Disorder. She was relieved to find she did not need medications for healing, and she embraced the self-care techniques her therapist offered. Ninety days in, her counselor suggested they had made major progress and would only need to see Janet on an as-needed basis. Janet's only disappointment was the sense she would miss the friendly and safe atmosphere of their weekly chats. Her therapist assured her that she would be available, if Janet felt it necessary.

Janet only consulted her therapist two times after that. She still thought of the elderly woman who would finish her life in a women's prison. But the numbness associated with the situation was gone and Janet wept for her as she prayed for Donna Franklin.

### Profiling Janet's Reactions

Compassion Fatigue, also known as Secondary Traumatic Stress, is a common reaction to regular exposure to uncommon situations. Becoming detached and cold to situations that would make others sad, often shows up in those who regularly work in crises. You never know what the next call will mean to your life.

For Janet, forgetting family functions, important dates, and tuning out the feelings of those closest to her were signs that her mind was failing to adequately deal with her ongoing and unusual stress.

## Questions to Consider

- **How do you feel about Janet's non-reaction to the older woman's arrest?**
- **Have you ever felt like the walls are closing in around you, and you don't know why?**
- **Do you see compassion fatigue and Janet's reaction as weakness or normal? Why or why not?**

## C.O.D.E. Conduct

**Communication** — Keeping things bottled up inside never solves problems — it's like shoveling the contents of a barn stall into a manure trailer. Sure, the stall looks good for a while, but you have to keep shoveling it out. At some point it will overflow, and the smell will become suffocating. Keep your soul-stall clean, communicate your feelings in a safe way with trusted people, journal your thoughts in a private notebook or computer file, or reach out to a credible, professional resource. Any of these practices can help protect you and your relationships from lasting harm.

**Objectiveness** — If you see compassion fatigue or secondary stress as weaknesses in others, think objectively about the possibility of its actual existence. Just for a moment consider: What if it is true? What if it could affect me? Is it affecting me now?

**Dedication** — It's a safety switch in a way. Each time you tell yourself that you've put your feelings in a metal box and forgotten them, or you let it go, those emotions never dissipate. Rather, they just continue to stack up in your mind, until they begin affecting other parts of your life. Resolve not to allow yourself to get away with this defensive tactic. Deal with your emotions often and early, so you don't suffer a bigger hit from them later.

**Engagement** — Learn more about Secondary Traumatic Stress and learn its true impact, so you can guard yourself and your family now — before it's too late. Pick up a book, talk to a counselor, listen to a podcast, research it on the web, or ask your department head to provide training. Take advantage of every opportunity to learn all you can about this stress issue.

## Law Enforcement Summary

Law enforcement officers wrestle perpetrators to the ground when they resist arrest. They dance the slow waltz of intensive interrogation — all hours of day and night. They chase Devil's Weed and Fentanyl-laced buttons down Heroine Highway. They knock on the doors of homicide victim's loved ones, obliged to deliver the worst of news.

They also help lost children find their way home and assist broken-down travelers on the side of the road. Whether it's working the major case squad or walking a rookie beat, cuffing an infamous criminal or writing a traffic ticket, the women and men of law enforcement are tasked with the responsibility to protect and serve the public.

When the big cases happen, those who wear the badge are forced to swim in oceans of adrenalin. They must digest abnormal doses of unusually high stress, deal with lack of sleep, and eating on the run, while attempting to maintain some sense of normalcy with family and friends. Through it all, their souls are often seared, especially when the court systems fail and special interest groups shout for their blood.

Our servants in blue are often under-appreciated, disrespected, and compensated with low pay, for the privilege of sacrificing so much. But still, there are rewards. Though not the outcome anyone truly hopes for, there is comfort in offering closure to a grieving family or solving a haunting case. Unearthing hidden facts when the obvious seems senseless, provides purpose and helps offset the mundane. Setting an example of integrity and purity for future generations, even if false accusations are raised, helps diminish the challenges to their purpose and effectiveness.

This section is dedicated to those who in the heat of dangerous moments, rush in to safeguard the well-being of all, regardless of race, gender, age, nationality, politics, or differing perspectives. Your willingness to perform your duties no matter what, are deeply appreciated. Thank you!

## Chapter 17
## Objective Overdose

A vibration in Jackson's pocket made his heart palpitate. *Not now,* he thought.

But Cen-Com's call refused denial. Jackson's job as Chief Deputy demanded first priority — though the father's heart that beat in Jackson's chest equally commanded his attention.

He looked toward Natalie, hunched in her defensive volleyball position, waiting for the competitor's serve. *How did she grow up so fast? How was it possible that she would turn seventeen next month?*

The ball spiked over the net, and Natalie deflected the ball to the setter. After her team successfully scored, she looked up and locked eyes with Jackson. It warmed his insides to know she still wanted her daddy's approval. He waved, and motioned that he had to leave.

Natalie's initial facial expression spoke the silent language of disappointment. But she masked it quickly with a smile and a shrug, before mouthing the words, "It's okay."

Jackson leaned over and kissed his wife on the cheek. "Gotta go. Cen-Com."

Allie offered her typical sunny southern admonishment. "Be careful and come home safe."

Jackson responded, "You know I will. Love you."

"Love you back," Allie's inner and outer beauty still caused Jackson's pulse to quicken. He had no idea that the case waiting for him would make this departure even harder after the fact.

Jackson pulled his deputy cruiser to a stop a few feet from the ambulance — lights blazing in red, yellow, and blue. In the yard, an eerie silence hung heavy, even the birds seemed to understand the need for solemnity. But a different atmosphere would soon slap Jackson in the face.

He exited his car quickly and glanced at his watch while he walked. Jackson made a mental note, *14:18 hours.*

He entered the home. Buzzing emergency responders

huddled in pods throughout the dwelling. Jackson followed their trail until he came to a doorway.

Jackson approached an EMS worker who stood on the fringe, while the Macon County coroner surveyed the body of a young woman. Her skin had already begun to blush violet-blue.

The EMS worker leaned close and whispered, "The victim is a seventeen-year-old female. Looks like an overdose, but the coroner hasn't called it yet. The family said they found her this way, and immediately tried CPR. "

Soured bile flooded Jackson's throat and seeped into his mouth. The deceased girl lay on the floor next to a bed covered in a rumpled, white frilly bedspread. Several opened notebooks with scrawls and scribbles, along with drawings depicting suicidal methods, scattered near an indentation resembling a human body. The carpet beneath the girl was covered in a drying pool of vomit. But something disturbed Jackson more than anything else he observed in the room.

The dead girl on the floor, favored his own Natalie.

Jackson mentally shook the conscious thought from his head, though the frothy foam coming from the mouth of the girl and lividity in her face and upper body, made the haunting resemblance to his daughter unsettling. Jackson had to regain a grip on the job at hand.

He inhaled, an exercise often practiced to increase clarity and focus on the job. "Was she originally lying face down in the bed?" Jackson directed his question to the EMS worker.

"The family confirmed that she was lying on the front side when they found her. They rolled her over and onto the floor."

A voice spoke reverently into Jackson's left ear. His fellow officer, Deputy Ben Dennis, said, "Chief, if you want to step outside, I'll advise you on the facts of the case as we know them."

The two men slipped away, but not before Jackson took another double-take of the child on the floor. *Why did she have to remind him so much of his own little girl?*

In the yard, Deputy Dennis read notes matter-of-factly

164

from his smart phone. "The mother of the home was preparing for a trip and went to get medication from their place of storage. She found bottles for Methocarbamol, Gabapentin, and Levathoraxen were missing. She immediately suspected her daughter may have taken them because of her history with depression and said she had suffered for a couple of years. According to the mother, the girl was showing some improvement with prescription assistance, but it was slow. An incident at school yesterday likely threw the girl into her suicidal state.

She had gotten in trouble at school and was suspended from the bus, as well as from school short term. The girl was caught by school officials performing oral sex on a boy while traveling on a bus to an art museum. The parents said they had a conversation with their daughter about the issue just prior to going to bed."

Jackson considered Natalie's naïveté and young age — then a fleeting thought made him wonder if he really knew his daughter. His stomach did a queasy somersault.

Deputy Dennis interrupted Jackson's discomforting thoughts. "This morning, when the mother discovered the missing medications, she went to her daughter's room. That's when she found her unresponsive and cold to the touch.

The first officer on the scene, observed three prescription bottle lids on the bed, but no bottles could be found to match. However, he did find an empty bottle for 800mg Ibuprofen hidden in a pile of stuffed toys suspended from the wall in a decorative net. We took photographs and will include them in the uploads section of the report."

Movement at the front door of the residence caught Jackson's attention. The coroner exited and approached he and Deputy Dennis. "Gentlemen," the coroner greeted them with a formal nod.

Jackson asked, "What are your initial findings?"

The coroner said, "I took the internal body temperature via liver probe at 06:40 hours and got the results after three minutes. The deceased body temperature was 93.8 degrees — the ambient room temperature was 71.4 degrees and the victim had been covered with a fleece blanket and dressed in night clothes. Upon closer examination, I found no other remarkable observation on the body. EMS on the scene gave me an ECG strip confirming Asystole. Unless other evidence appears to contradict, I'd say it's an obvious suicide.

I contacted the child abuse and neglect hotline to report the death. I'll update my report when I have autopsy and toxicology information to add. Such an unfortunate case." He dropped a heavy hand on Jackson's shoulder, before walking away, head lowered.

Deputy Dennis excused himself as well, leaving Jackson to contend with his muddled emotions. *What if the girl lying inside was his child? Wouldn't he want someone to be there for her to ensure she was treated with dignity and care? And yet he was torn, because he had a little girl of his own who needed him to be there to support her, to talk to her and to attend her events.*

This case had stirred something deep inside Jackson — concerns he'd avoided crept to the surface of his conscious mind. It wasn't going to be easy, but an epiphany made Jackson realize change was necessary. A parent only gets an average of eighteen summers with their child, Natalie's seventeenth birthday was coming soon.

He couldn't change the mistakes he'd made in his past, but he could become intentional in his present and future. Somehow he must determine how to remain objective when writing his reports on this disturbing death. Today's investigation would force him to confront some things he'd long been ignoring with his daughter.

## Profiling Jackson's Reactions

A blindsiding trigger can derail any of us. In Jackson's situation, the young lady's suicide awakened the reality that Daddy's little girl has grown up, and he may not know her as well as he would like. What if she harbored secrets that put her in danger? A fresh start was needed.

## Questions to Consider

- **What would help Jackson maintain his objectivity when reporting the facts of the girl's suicide who reminded him so much of his Natalie?**
- **How should he best approach his fears in a healthy way, allowing him to bridge communication lapses that had become habitual in his daughter's teen years?**
- **What would help Jackson focus on balancing his work and home life?**

## C.O.D.E. Conduct

**Communication** — Talk with people who can relate and truly understand what you have experienced. Sharing emotions with people who get it, can speed up the healing process for everyone involved.

**Objectiveness** — Doing your job does not require robotic disconnectedness. You can feel empathy for others while still doing your job professionally and effectively.

**Dedication** — Help others memorialize those who died. Take up a cause or start a new one that invests in the living, as a way to honor the dying. Don't allow survivor's guilt or "why" questions to devour you. Use your emotional energy to support those who are dealing with fresh grief or sorrow.

**Engagement** — Plan some time for self-care and relational tending. Allow what you've been through to strengthen bonds and deepen appreciation for your relationships.

## Chapter 18
## Pennies on the Robbery

It was Louise's first day as a homicide detective — she felt wired and fired up — ready to tackle the job she'd worked so hard to get. Louise had no idea that her first day would bring her first case and one that challenge her sanity.

Veteran Dennis Hollis, was teaching Louise how to fill out her first search warrant request. Hollis emphasized the importance of details. "Pay attention Henderson, you miss one small point, it could be thrown out of court and cost the prosecution our case."

His finger was still resting on one of the required spaces when the phone interrupted his instruction. "Hollis," he said into the charcoal gray receiver.

Louise took note of the detective's brisk tone. Anyone on the other end of the line would know he was a man in charge with no time to waste. *Particularly as a woman, I need to look and sound that confident, even if I don't feel it,* Louise reminded herself. *But I'm sure solving over 300 murders doesn't hurt his self-esteem.*

"We're on the way." Detective Hollis snatched his suit jacket off the back of the chair at the same time he laid down the phone. "Let's go, Rookie. You just got lucky. Robbery and homicide at a grocery store on Juarez Street. One confirmed fatality and another victim barely hanging on. You get to go from being a newbie to an old hand in the span of about fifteen minutes. Not everyone gets OTJT their first day."

"OTJT?" Louise instantly berated herself for allowing the question to spill off her lips. *Now you really look stupid,* she thought.

But Hollis didn't seem to mind and didn't make fun of her

as he led the way out of the precinct, taking long strides toward their unmarked car. "Sorry, hazard of decades-long duty. I sometimes forget people don't know what they don't know. Means on the job training."

Louise nodded her acknowledgement as they faced each other while simultaneously buckling their seat belts. "Good to know," she added.

They drove in silence while the siren wailed and lights flashed above their heads. Dennis Hollis drove like a Nascar® driver, but his obvious experience behind the wheel made Louise feel secure and safe. Her mind drifted to imaginings of what her first homicide scene might hold.

When they screeched to a stop, Louise noted the large group of neighbors and onlookers, as well as a couple of press vans already on site. But her attention was quickly diverted as Hollis hopped out of the car and hurdled the steps leading into the small corner grocery. Louise hustled to keep up.

One of the first things Louise noted was the odd behavior of the family. They were unquestionably Asian by their facial features and the hushed language they spoke amongst themselves. But all five people were turned away from the scene where EMS was working on what appeared to be a middle-aged woman, tiny in stature, and in obvious medical distress.

*Maybe they're really squeamish about blood,* Louise thought.

Hollis leaned over and whispered to Louise, "We need to get their statements. But prepare yourself, it won't be easy. In their culture, this is considered a bad death."

"Bad death?" Louise realize she spoke louder than she meant to, and louder than appropriate.

Detective Hollis again overlooked her rookie mistake. He

whispered again. "In many Asian cultures, a bad death is defined by certain dates, suicide, or murder. They are not allowed to look on the deceased if a bad death occurs."

Louise lowered her voice to Hollis's decibel. "So how will we get an identification on the victim?"

"Someone will show up. They always do."

As if beckoned from a side stage, a voice echoed from the front door. "Can I help with anything? I'm Mr. and Mrs. Ying's neighbor."

"There's your cue, go get his statement," Hollis said.

Louise went to meet the mystery man.

The neighbor was blonde, green-eyed, about 6'2", and attractive. Louise immediately focused on his words.

"I wasn't gone very long. I work second shift, and I ran out to grab some coffee this morning at Art & Joe's Cafe. I usually check in on the Ying's first thing, but I woke up late today. I grew up next to them. The house I live in was my mom and dad's, I inherited it. Mr. and Mrs. Ying have been like a second set of grandparents. I came to the store every day, ever since I can remember. Their kids are my close friends. Are they going to be okay? Do you know what happened? Do you have any suspects? What kind of evidence have you found? How can I help?"

There it was, the reason for Louise's mental red flag. *Why is he so interested in suspects and evidence? And he seems overly anxious to help.* All in good time, Mr. ?"

"Sanders. Lance Sanders."

Detective Hollis walked from the back of the store and motioned Louise aside.

"Don't go anywhere, Mr. Sanders. I'll be back in a few minutes," she said

"Okay," Sanders didn't act like someone who'd just lost *a second set of grandparents.*

Hollis updated Louise on his initial findings. "The till is forced open. See if you can get one of the Ying children to go outside with you, so you can interview them."

"But I thought you said they wouldn't cooperate."

"Louise, you need to listen to the details. Good listening skills can solve a case — poor ones can flush one down the toilet. I told you they won't view the deceased family member if they've had a bad death. I never said they wouldn't cooperate."

"I understand." Louise felt like a fourteen-year-old admonished for not doing her homework. She turned toward the line of adult Ying children and their spouses, neatly lined up in order of birth, backs facing their parents.

A groan echoed from deeper inside the store. Louise instinctually glanced in the noise's direction. She found it odd that even in her peripheral vision, she could tell the Ying children did not move.

She approached a young man who looked to be in his early to mid-thirties. "Might I have a word with you? Outside?"

He didn't answer verbally, but nodded his head once, in a polite affirmative. He stepped toward Louise, and his wife followed automatically.

"I'm sorry, I need you four to wait here. We'll just be a few minutes, then I'd like to speak with each of you as well."

Their reaction was unexpected.

All of their faces looked stricken, but the daughter spoke. "No. Please do not say that number. It is bad luck to speak it in the presence of the ill. Our mother." The young woman pointed to her sister-in-law. "And she must go with you and my brother."

Louise was confused. "Excuse me? What did I say? I need to interview you separately, so it's important that the rest of you wait here."

The young woman stiffened. "It must not be so. If you speak to my brother alone, we must split up. My younger brother and my husband will wait out by the car. My sister-in-law will stand here with me."

"But if you will give me a few minutes with your brother, I'll come and get the rest of you, one at a time."

The younger woman's voice became forceful. "No. It is bad luck. My father already has a bad death. Please, do not cause my mother to have a bad death, too."

Louise opened her mouth to ask more questions, but Lance Sanders spoke first. "Can I speak with you outside, officer?"

*What now?* Louise thought. *This guy's up to something.* She nodded for Sanders to lead so she could follow.

As soon as they stepped onto the street, he said, "The number four is what they are talking about. In their culture, any occurrence or mention of the number four in the presence of the ill or injured, is bad luck and could lead to a bad death. For the Ying children, they've already lost their dad to a bad death, because it was murder. If they lose their mom because four of them are left standing together, then they would feel responsible for her bad death. It's a taboo where they come from."

Louise had to admit, the guy made sense. But Lance Sanders was a still a suspect in her mind. She thanked him and went back inside.

"Okay, if you two would go outside and wait by the car," Louise pointed to the youngest son and his brother-in-law. "You two wait here," she nodded at the daughter and wife of the oldest son. Then she escorted the oldest brother out the front door.

Her interview was fruitful. The son said, "I worked earlier

this morning, and went home for an early lunch while Dad and Mom worked the store. There was only thirty-seven dollars in the cash register when I left, I had counted it shortly before I left. My house is next door, the house on the other side of Lance's. I keep an eye on my parents, they're getting older, you know." He wiped moisture from the edge of his eye.

"I only saw one couple walk toward the store, and they didn't look like they had much to spend. She was white with bright red hair, and she didn't walk so much as she shuffled her feet. The man was dark skinned. Maybe Latino or a light-skinned black man. I'm not sure which."

"Tell me about Lance," Louise pressed, more interested in him than a couple who probably bought a pack of smokes and six pack of beer.

"We grew up together. He's a good guy. Someone you can count on, you know? Helps out a lot."

Louise thought, *I'm pretty sure he helped himself more than he helped you.*

After she finished with the oldest son, Louise interviewed the rest of the family. The wife of the oldest confirmed his story, but had little to offer about who Louise was most interested in — Lance.

Louise was speaking with the youngest son, when the mother was rushed out on a gurney. Hollis hadn't exaggerated how she looked. The young man brushed her hand as the paramedics pushed her fast toward the back of the ambulance. He said, "I love you, Mother." Then he looked toward the ground.

Like his sister and brother-in-law, he had no relevant information to add.

Louise found Hollis stepping from behind the register, his gloved hands empty. He pointed at the cash drawer. "If it was a theft, they only got pennies on the robbery. Two lives lost, for less than a meal at most restaurants. Such a waste."

"Maybe it wasn't a robbery. What if the killer is trying to cover something else up? And did the woman die?" Louise said.

"No, she's still hanging on."

"But you said two lives lost."

"You saw how badly she was beaten. Her face is unrecognizable, she has a compound fracture in her left arm, and who knows how much internal damage. If she survives, she'll never be the same. Tragic."

Louise nodded her head. "Well, the neighbor is intriguing. He has an unusual interest in evidence and suspects."

"Evidence?"

"Just his demeanor and questions."

"Certainly could mean something, but it's not hard evidence."

"Don't a lot of perpetrators come back to the scene and try to involve themselves in the investigation? To distract and spin the direction?"

"Sure. But not everyone interested in helping and getting more information is guilty. Evidence, Henderson. Not everything is as it first appears."

She felt like that insecure teenager again — hands slapped. It became worse days later when the facts of the case led to the real culprits of the heinous crime.

Hollis told her the red-headed woman and her Hispanic boyfriend had robbed the store and beaten the Ying's. "All for nine lousy dollars." They had confessed in minutes, after they were arrested. One of their neighbors turned them in, after the couple had offered to sell them an ornate Asian pin. The woman had lifted it off of Mrs. Ying, and after beating her with a hammer, she picked off a back shelf in the store. Her boyfriend had murdered Mr. Ying.

Louise dropped her face in her hands. "I messed everything up. I offended the family. I didn't follow the evidence trail."

Hollis gave her a reassuring tap on the shoulder. "Happens to the best, starting out."

Louise looked up and rubbed her temples. "I mentally convicted the Sanders guy and stopped listening. You warned me."

"It's part of the learning curve, Henderson. You're learning. And there is one piece of good news. Sounds like Mrs. Ying is going to make a miraculous recovery. She's going to live with some disabilities from the beating, but from what I've been told, she will survive. They have a strong family, so they have hope."

*Hope,* Louise thought. *I almost stole their hope.*

A few months later, surprising visitors came to see Louise and Hollis at the station. Mrs. Ying still wore the wounds from her beating, but she was healing faster than Louise would have imagined. The Ying children, all five, stood with her. The oldest son stepped forward and bowed slightly.

"We want to thank you, for saving our mother."

Louise objected. "That was the paramedics, doctors, and nurses. We did nothing."

"Ah, but you did. You respected our wishes and allowed us our dignity. Because of you, we did not have bad luck after our mother was injured." He placed a gentle arm around his mother. "Because of you, she is with us today. We did not lose both of our parents to a bad death. Thank you."

The entire family bowed at the waist in sequence and they turned in unison, leaving Louise standing in awe of their appreciation.

## Profiling Louise's Reactions

Louise's reactions to a new job, new circumstances and a different culture is completely normal. You can expect to err while you learn, but a listening ear will lessen bad consequences. Though she made some rookie mistakes, Louise did not let them sideline her. In the end she was able to see that she truly helped a distressed family in need.

## Questions to Consider

- **Have you ever made rookie mistakes? What happened as a result?**
- **How many times have you let yourself predetermine the facts before you had the evidence to back your judgment up? What could that have cost?**
- **What cases have you worked where cultural diversity, race, nationality, gender, or other differences impacted the methods used in your investigation or other emergency services efforts?**

## C.O.D.E. Conduct

**Communication** — Never be afraid to ask questions or seek clarification. Be open to new ideas and differing perspectives. If you don't understand or agree with something you are told — repeat what you thought you heard, asking the speaker to confirm or clarify their message. You might discover something surprising.

**Objectiveness** — From the first day to the last, you will never reach a state of "knowing it all." Don't feel ashamed when you discover you didn't know what you didn't know. Accept learning from others as an opportunity, instead of a threat.

**Dedication** — You will feel embarrassed or inadequate at times, it's part of the human condition. However, acting with integrity (doing the same thing whether you believe anyone else can see or hear you, or not), will carry you through. Dedicate yourself to embracing the learning curve, it's a must in this line of work.

**Engagement** — Seek out those who have gone before you, talk with them and listen for their wisdom. Don't discount anything as old school or out of date, sometimes their experiences are crucial to present-day solutions. After all, learning from others' hard lessons, can pave the way for a more productive future.

# Chapter 19
## After Sirens Wail

Fresh off duty, Sam Chavez noted the darkening May sky. She was mesmerized by the odd, low-lying milky-green swirl shrouded in a steel gray cloud. She flipped on the radio, twisting the dial to the local news station, but keeping the volume low, so it didn't interfere with any calls from dispatch.

The radio reporter's voice changed as he announced, from controlled to strained. He said, "This is a tornado emergency. This is higher than a tornado warning. This is the most significant warning we can give. If you live in Moore, you need to take cover in a storm shelter now. Do not hesitate, do not wait, move below ground immediately."

Sam looked back up at the sky and she didn't like what she saw. She briskly turned the news off, then pushed the button on her police radio. She gave Cen-Com her number before reporting, "I'm at the corner of Fourth and Pennsylvania Avenue. I've got rotation above my head to the west."

In an instant, Cen-Com responded with information from one of Chavez's fellow officers in another location. As the two-mile-wide monster ground its way through Moore, the minutes seemed to pass in slow motion while simultaneously making Sam feel as if she was moving at warp speed. Throughout the afternoon, she and other officers tried to stay out of each other's way while reporting real-time on what they could see from their location.

As the monster churned, Sam's siren harmonized with the tornado sirens blaring around her. Her mind strayed to her husband, Paul, and the kids. She had called Paul and told him to get in their shelter, but her husband was already en route to pick up their daughter, Priscilla. She hadn't been able to reach him when she tried to call back to make sure they were safe.

It would be over an hour before she found out her child and husband were trapped in the collapsed school building.

But while the storm raged, as debris assaulted the city, Sam remained in an adrenalin soup of mixed emotions — fear for her family's safety swirled with the professional demands to take care of others.

The tornadic devil plowed through twenty miles of Moore's landscape. Sam, like others on the front line of emergency services, followed and watched from a safe distance, pushing family to the back burner of her mind. Finally, the tornado's rope dissipated. It took a few minutes for Sam to grasp everything that had happened, even with the carnage right in front of her. But all of her emotions heightened again when Cen-Com announced, "All available officers, please proceed to Briarwood Elementary School at 149th and Western."

Winding her way around overturned vehicles, downed electric poles, shards of metal, glass, and other debris left by the tornado, Sam's progress felt like a crawl. As she drove past a concrete slab, it didn't immediately register that it had been the 7-11 store she was so familiar with. Rows of what had been beautiful brick homes were now heaped into unrecognizable mountains of rubble. As she drove, Sam could see people beginning to climb out from under masses of debris and twisted lumber.

Finally, Sam came to the end of the street and she rolled her window down to wave a fire truck and ambulance through the maze. The sounds of victims crying for help echoed through her patrol car. She knew many of them were stuck in their storm shelters or beneath heavy debris, but she couldn't stop. Other rescue workers were arriving and would assist, but Sam continued on. The last known location of Paul and Priscilla was at Briarwood. She had to get to her husband and child.

When Sam screeched to a stop in the school parking lot, she couldn't believe it was the same place she'd come hundreds of times to pick up Priscilla. The smell of freshly churned earth assaulted Sam's senses. The entire building was flattened. Sam forced herself to swallow the thick bile creeping up her throat.

Shrill screams of panicked parents filled the air. And a

steady stream of adults leading crying children, climbed out of the decimated structure. It seemed unlikely that anyone could have survived.

Sam jumped from her car and sprinted toward the exodus of survivors. All thoughts of her uniform dissolved as she desperately joined other parents, shouting their children's names. "Priscilla! Paul! Priscilla!" she howled.

She made it into a darkened hallway, and paused to try and get her bearings. "Where is Priscilla's class?" she muttered to herself. Then she spotted a large piece of tattered red construction paper with yellow stars flapping in the post-storm breeze. Sam knew what it was instantly, and she ran toward the doorway next to it.

Shoving splintered desks aside, Sam shrieked, "Paul, Priscilla, are you in here?"

A muffled voice answered, but not from inside the room she was standing in. "Sam? We're here. We're here."

Sam turned and rushed out of the doorway, then she abruptly stopped from shock. With blood oozing from the left side of his face, Sam's husband limped toward her, clutching their daughter tightly at his side. Other than mussed hair and tears, their little girl appeared to be all right. Sam broke into a run again.

After a thorough exam at the hospital, Sam was relieved to learn that Paul and Priscilla were both going to be fine. Sadly, some of the parents whose children attended nearby Plaza Towers Elementary School, did not get the same type of report.

Sam gripped her husband's hand after Priscilla was in bed that evening, while they watched the local news. The man reporting on Plaza Towers Elementary lost his composure as he said, "We're told it is no longer a rescue mission, but a recovery effort. Authorities say they're going to pull the tiny victims out of the rubble here shortly. But. . . ." His voice cracked and trailed off, in a moment of lost words.

Sam knew a dome of silence filled the air when the rescue workers realized they couldn't reach victims in time. What she didn't know was how long her paranoia and the recurrent survivor's guilt would haunt her over the trauma her community endured that day.

The EF-5 tornado chewed the ground for thirty-nine minutes that day. It caused billions of dollars in damage and claimed twenty-four lives. Seven were children. Sam struggled with feelings of responsibility because of the fatalities in her city, especially when she thought of the lost children.

Ultimately, it took several weeks of intensive work with a grief counselor to help Sam come to terms with the historic act of nature that ripped through her community. But she also leaned into the resilience of her family, neighbors, and fellow emergency workers — tough Oklahomans. They lived out the philosophy of, "You last, and everyone else first." They mourned together, and eventually, learned to rejoice together. In togetherness, Sam experienced true healing.

For months after that sad, May day, on a street Sam often patrolled, a tattered American flag waved from a stump of a broken tree. Its bright colors rippled in the wind against a stark and desolate, brown background. But the flag spoke encouragement, inspiration, and hope to Sam's hurting heart.

At a stoplight one day, Sam looked in the mirror and smiled at the woman who grinned back. The sky was clear and her family was safe — no matter what the job brought or how the sirens wailed, as long as Paul and Priscilla were okay, it was going to be a great day. Life became a matter of perspective.

## Profiling Sam's Reactions

Like many who work in emergency services fields, under pressure, Sam experienced an internal communication struggle. In her case, her human instinct was to run to find her family, but she also had a strong sense of duty to her profession. Her dilemma called for strict self-discipline, not easy when the people you love the most are in the clutches of immediate peril. After all, what comes first, the job or family?

Sam demonstrated commitment to her job and family when she bravely engaged in grief counseling, so she could come to terms with the destruction in her community and loss of children. She also needed help in working through the survivor's guilt she felt, since her child was spared, when others were not. Sam became more effective on the job, by giving herself permission to work through her mental fatigue and stress.

## Questions to Consider

- **How do you keep calm and maintain professionalism when your worst fears may be realized?**
- **When does survivor's guilt hit people? What kinds of situations cause survivor's guilt?**
- **What circumstances might be so troubling that a grief counselor is needed to help a person work through their feelings?**

## C.O.D.E. Conduct

**Communication** — The unknown often spurs the most powerful fear a human being can feel. But panic is not a luxury available to those who sacrifice time and energy with their families, to protect and care for others. This is why it's important to talk yourself through fear in the midst of a crisis, waiting for an appropriate time and place for facing your feelings, when the job is complete.

**Objectiveness** — Remaining objective while riding out storms, literal or emotional, is crucial to surviving. Reminding yourself that 97% of what humans fear never happens can help you maintain a logical perspective when you feel like collapsing under worry and fear. It takes courage, strength, and resolve to look at situations with potential personal consequences, and not let unreliable emotions cloud your judgment.

**Dedication** — Everyone working in emergency services has taken some form of a sworn oath to protect others, even if there is a great risk to self-interests. At times, family must come first, as they should. But dedication requires sacrifice, meaning sometimes, family comes after someone else. Evaluating appropriateness in each individual situation is necessary if you want healthy family relationships, while proving your loyalty to your career choice.

**Engagement** — Doing a job where you see people at their worst, while worrying about your family, friends, and neighborhood, can cause you to shut down emotionally. It might seem easier to disconnect than to wrestle with fears of losing someone who matters a great deal to you. But if you give in to this temptation, you end up missing out on the greatest gifts of life. Yes, there are risks in opening up your soul to others, but if you put a wall up, you won't experience some of life's blessings: laughter, intimacy, companionship, joy, and freedom.

## Chapter 20
## Final Impact

John Castellano bolted upright, shaken from his nightmare-ridden sleep. Sticky sweat covered John's forehead and upper lip as his body attempted to cool the heated flush of his face. He pulled his knees to his chest and looked around the apartment. *How is this my life?*

Only a few weeks before, John had been trying to understand who he'd become. *Why can I remember in vivid detail, every scene I've ever worked, but when it comes to family matters, I struggle to recall important events?* The consequences caught up with him, after John failed to make his wife's promotion party on time. She hit the ceiling. The smoldering daggers in her eyes told him things would be unpleasant when they got home. He was right.

John pulled into the driveway ahead of his wife. Without glancing in his direction, Darla slammed her car door and marched inside. He trailed her in silence.

Once in the door, Darla threw her purse on the counter and said, "I want a divorce. I'm done. And these are not idle words this time, John. I mean it. I'm calling a lawyer tomorrow."

John felt the air exit his lungs. "Babe, I'm sorry. I don't know what's wrong with me. I'll work on it, I promise."

"I've heard your promises before, but instead of things getting better, they're getting worse. The kids feel like they've lost their father, and I haven't had a husband in a long time. You're worthless to this family. We'll be better off without you."

Darla's words caused John's legs to buckle, the full weight

of his body held up only by the counter he leaned against. John's wife had validated his secret fears. In a single exchange, his marriage was over.

Seven months after their separation, John's work related flashbacks, erratic up until then, came more often and were getting worse. Now, they were affecting his daytime thoughts and stifling his ability to function. As he sat in the bed after yet another nightmare, a thousand thoughts pummeled his mind. He got up, grabbed a notebook and ink pen, and began to write.

*Twenty-seven years of trauma. Holding dying babies in my arms. Pulling mangled bodies from vehicles. Seeing the horrific methods monsters will use to murder people. Holding the hands of women and men as the last light of life fades from their bodies, lying when they ask me if they'll be all right. These have filled the majority of my waking hours for most of my adult life.*

*I've viewed tragedies of all sorts and countless suicides. I've fed the homeless and sheltered the abused, only to have some turn and attack me for my efforts. I've helped kids who had nothing see the possibility of something better in their futures. I missed family birthdays and Christmases, hospital visits and school sports. When I felt overwhelmed, I drove to someplace dark and cried. Alone.*

*Through it all, I've prayed for people I don't even know. I wear the badge to protect and serve for low pay and little respect, but who's here to help me face my pain? Who cares about what I feel? Who's praying for me?*

*It's getting harder and harder to stuff the reality of what I've seen and heard into the recesses of my subconscious. My wife is right, the world would be better off if I were dead.*

*I'm sorry I'm such a failure. Please forgive me, Darla,*

*Abby, Cam, and Freddie.*

John signed his name, but he tucked it into the nightstand drawer. A part of him wanted to end it all immediately, but he had his family to consider. He needed to think through some things and wanted to get his affairs in order before he was ready to call it quits.

John swung his legs to the side of the bed and drew his hands to his face, rubbing up and down as if to wipe away the anxiety racking his mind. When the motions didn't alleviate his emotional angst, John pushed himself into a standing position and stumbled to the bathroom. He splashed cold water on his face, neck, and ears, not bothering to towel off. He could hardly stand to look at himself in the mirror anymore.

His mental state perpetuated a familiar monologue of dark self-talk.

*You are worthless. You can't do anything right these days. You suck as a husband and dad. You're not holding it together like you used to. Face it, Darla and the kids would have a better life if they collected your life insurance.*

John looked toward the ceiling. "God, if you're real, I sure could use a sign down here."

Then he scoffed, inwardly chastising himself for his foolishness. *What's the point? You should just off yourself — like Cash did.*

Weeks before, Cash Roberts had written a suicide note to his family, left it on his kitchen table, then took his service revolver, placed it inside his mouth, and pulled the trigger. No one in their department had guessed that Cash was struggling. He had an easy laugh, joking often, even though he was going through a divorce like John.

In the wee hours of the morning, John couldn't help comparing his own life to that of his fallen brother.

Every aspect of John's existence felt broken: relationally, emotionally, financially, mentally, spiritually, and now all of it was impacting him physically. Every day he buckled under a motivational deficit — his drive was gone.

John wondered if Cash had wrestled in similar ways.

As he reflected, John could now identify subtle signs of Cash's cover up. In the weeks preceding his death, Cash had refused all social invitations, offering shallow excuses. John was doing the same.

Occasionally, Cash had a distant look in his eyes and seemed unusually distracted when someone asked him a question. He was slow in responding most of the time.

Lately, John's co-workers were beginning to accuse him of reacting in kind, calling him "slow" and asking, "What's up with you lately?"

Cash also appeared to have lost some mental acuteness on the job, taking longer to document evidence and put facts together. John's own mental fog was hindering his efficiency.

Though Cash continued to laugh a lot, he did have increasing moments of snappish behavior — snarling unreasonably and at inappropriate times. John's colleagues would probably accuse him of acting rudely without cause. His lack of rest and increasing worry were taking their toll on his mood.

The day before Cash died, there was a particularly odd exchange between the two.

Cash and John were standing at the edge of a crime scene, when without any reason John could comprehend, Cash had asked, "Do you believe in Heaven?"

Feeling uncomfortable and unsure how to answer, John hesitated.

Cash filled the silence. "I mean, do you believe there's a God. This all-seeing, all-knowing, all-understanding-even-though-nothing-seems-to-make-sense-to-us, God."

John drew a deep breath into his lungs. He sensed this was a moment for full transparency and not macho BS. "Well, actually I do. Don't get me wrong, there's a lot I don't grasp, especially some of the things we see on this job. But when I look at the patterns in nature, like plants and animals on land having a similar design as things in the deep ocean or in outer space, I can't buy into random cells organizing so masterfully.

I think there's a lot more factual evidence supporting intelligent design than accidental evolution. Even some of the hard cases we deal with point to a Master Creator, especially when coincidences lead to convictions."

Cash had tilted his head in contemplation. "Do you think he really forgives people. No matter what they've done."

John felt completely unqualified and awkward. "I'm not a pastor, rabbi, or priest, but I guess so. I've always been told if we asked him to forgive us he would."

"Even if we hurt our families? Or ourselves?"

"Maybe you should talk to someone who knows more than I do. Me and Darla aren't doing too hot right now, so I'm probably not the right guy to give you any guidance. I can't get my own act together, and I sure don't have God figured out."

A slight blush had tinged Cash's cheeks. "Sorry. I didn't mean to put you on the spot."

"You didn't. And I'm not trying to brush you off. If you really need to talk. . . ."

Cash had interrupted. "I'm fine. Really." Then he offered up his familiar grin. "I'll figure things out. Probably overthinking all of it anyway. After all, what's the point?"

John shuddered in remembrance of the relief he had felt, as well as the tone in which Cash said, "What's the point?" It hadn't matched the smile on his face. But it did match the emotional tone in John's thoughts, when he silently asked himself the same kind of question.

For a few lingering moments, John analyzed his similarities with Cash, even allowing himself to consider Cash's choice as justification for his own suicidal temptations. But there were elements in that last conversation with Cash that stopped him.

John wondered, *If God and Heaven are real, how would suicide affect his afterlife?*

The images of Cash's parents and siblings at his friend's funeral washed all other thoughts out of John's mind. He remembered his own pain as he sat numbly through the service. He saw Cash's estranged wife and children, sobbing as they mourned. Then his thoughts shifted.

John's imagination took him to his own funeral, where he saw his own parents and siblings wiping away tears. His favorite uncle would undoubtedly be there. The crowd of men and women from the force, fresh from Cash's memorial, would wear the same stark expressions stretched over clenched jaws.

Though he wanted to dismiss his thoughts, John forced himself to honestly confront reality. He allowed himself to envision the faces of Darla and his own children. Then the questions began.

*What would it do to my parents if I gave up? How would Darla and the kids truly feel if I took my own life? Cash's family is definitely not better off. His children will bear the stigma of their father's death all of their days.*

*Those of us who worked with him aren't faring well either — for the past week, everyone's been wearing haunted expressions, and I know we're all thinking about him.*

John pondered, *Does my current pain compare to the suffering I'll cause others if I choose to die? Did Cash's?*

In those pre-dawn hours, John allowed himself to accept truthful answers to his questions. He well understood the level of his vulnerability. Statistically, copycat suicides spiked during the week after a person took their life. The numbers climbed even higher among those who personally identified with the victim.

These notions were enough to carry John through to daylight. It was enough. Within hours, he would experience something he felt was the sign he had asked God for — an affirmation telling him, *Regardless of how you feel, fight as courageously to save your own life as you would for someone else's.*

John pinched the bridge of his nose to remove the sleepless crust from his eyes as he drove to the precinct. He blinked twice to clear the matting, just in time to catch a peripheral view of a car careening out of control. John mentally mapped its probable course, horrified to note the car's zig-zagging, propelling it toward a school playground full of children. John's training triggered instantly.

He pushed the accelerator to the floorboard, simultaneously surveying the landscape and traffic. Only one course of action made sense, so John angled his vehicle based on the trajectory of the approaching car.

When the other vehicle struck, the impact shoved John's vehicle horizontally over two parking curbs, but after all motion stopped, both automobiles rested several feet from the protective fencing around the school yard.

John's adrenal rush shook him from his stunned state and helped him get out of his vehicle. The figure behind the steering wheel of the car that had crashed into him was slumped and unmoving.

John moved in for a closer inspection cautiously, and he could see a gray-haired female with a small stream of blood dripping from her nose.

He called the situation in, requesting an ambulance dispatch to his location. It was only after he hung up, that John heard the energetic shouts and clanking metal of the fence as it vibrated beneath excited young hands.

"Did you see that?"

"Are you okay, Mister?"

"Is that lady dead?"

"Wow! It was just like the movies."

The calming influence of an adult voice spoke. "Come along now, children. We need to get back to class. There's nothing more to see." A small swarm of women and men ushered the students away from the fence and into the building, successfully moving them inside, mere minutes before the sirens and lights arrived.

Later, John found out the elderly woman was having a heart attack, and unable to control her car. She likely would have injured many children that day. Because of his quick thinking, not only were the students spared, but the woman survived as well.

In the following days, every time John replayed the scene, he better understood the difference two blinks had made. And he vowed not to ever take his life for granted again.

John didn't care for the public accolades, nor did he like to hear people call him a hero, but in his private pondering, John did acknowledge the fact that his actions had mattered. If he had killed himself in the hours prior, as he had contemplated, several innocent children could have died.

A local news reporter said of John's actions, "His ripple in the pond of life will spread for generations." Something about that statement inspired John to take another brave step.

John sought professional counseling for his recurring nightmares and inner demons — realizing that strength, not weakness, motivated those who sought help. He also went to Darla and opened up in ways that made him feel very vulnerable, more for his own healing than in any hopes for reconciliation. But after his wife realized John was sincere and not merely making surface attempts to manipulate her feelings, a miracle occurred.

Darla, hungry for her husband's affection, responded with an open heart.

After several months of learning more about each other's personalities, life influences, and expectations, along with training on specific communication techniques, they began to fall deeper in love. Together, they saved their marriage.

John also learned how to process his job-related emotions in a healthy way, allowing him the energy and focus to care for his personal life in a balanced way. His professional work improved dramatically as well.

When John released himself from the prison of pride, by opening up to others, he unlocked the door to freedom and peace. By breaking out of his inner barriers, he discovered the secret to living healthy, happy, and whole while submerged in trauma, tragedy, and death. He later tore his suicide note into tiny pieces and burned it on a cool, spring day. John had reasons to live.

## Profiling John's Reactions

When life is going wrong, the temptation to give up can be great. The voice telling you, *Just check out. It will be easier on you and everyone you care about,* is dangerous, and seductive.

Refuse to listen to the emotional lies born from years of stress, trauma and tragedy, in a world where dark melancholy shadows try to cover your soul. Let midnight thoughts melt into the sunrise of hope.

Like John learned, you can turn off those emotional lies and listen to the voice of truth which affirms, *You are important. You matter. The world is better because you exist.*

Your efforts are making a difference for someone, even when you can't see the results. We need more brave people in the world like you, who stand up and do right, who work with ethics and integrity, and who put others before themselves, sacrificing self for a greater good.

### Questions to Consider

- **Reflect back on your career and personal life, was there ever a time where your actions directly saved someone else from harm? What might have happened had you not been there?**
- **How does a suicide increase the odds of others following suit? Have you ever contemplated suicide?**
- **Why do you think the statistics for divorce and suicide are so high for those who work in emergency services fields? How can you protect your relationships?**

### C.O.D.E. Conduct

**Communication** — Anytime you have thoughts of giving up and checking out, especially if someone near you has taken their life, do the opposite of instinct, which is to keep your thoughts secret. Run to the confidence of a trusted person and tell them what you are feeling and thinking — a counselor or therapist, a chaplain, pastor, priest, or rabbi, an anonymous call line, a stress management agency, a family member, or friend. Tell them about your struggles.

**Objectiveness** — When your emotions suggest that people will be better off if you are gone or that no one cares, consider the facts. If there is even one family member, friend, co-worker, organization, or association you have a relationship with, then you can be assured your life matters to someone. Your smile, kind gesture, or prayer makes a difference to others — including strangers — even if you don't see a direct result yourself. Watch the classic movie, *It's a Wonderful Life*, but from a student's point of view. You aren't George Bailey, but guaranteed, you were created on purpose in order to fulfill a purpose. You may not value what you contribute, but others do. Think factually and objectively about how life would be different if you were not around.

**Dedication** — Instead of allowing yourself to focus on what you don't have or wallow about the things gone wrong, dedicate yourself to counting blessings. This is more than an old adage, the saying has been around so long, simply because it makes life more bearable on difficult days.

**Engagement** — Whatever mistakes you made yesterday or even five minutes ago — they are in the past. Today, in this moment, you have the opportunity to grab life with fresh gusto, to act with fresh faith in humanity and the sanctity of life. To do your job with fresh passion. To show compassion to your fellow man and woman. People are watching you — your family, your co-workers, your community. Choose to be a catalyst for courage, inspiring others to follow an example you would want them to emulate.

# Epilogue

Whether your case is weather, terrorist, or kitten-in-a-tree related, everything you do matters to someone. You have the ability to save and improve the quality of numerous lives — you are called to a special task that few can do.

Many who work in emergency services fields will not admit they need help or ask for it, because they are afraid of appearing weak or fearful of losing their jobs. When your life is spiraling out of control, when the world you're infused in and the circumstances around you have become too big for you to handle, you will be tempted to internalize your fears and pain. But danger lurks if you choose that path — we don't keep secrets, secrets keep us — bound in bondage.

No matter what you are facing, never ignore the options available for help or the fact that you are needed. You are needed!

Your family needs you, the people you serve need you, and the world needs you. Don't allow your feelings to rule over you. Act in spite of your emotions, until what you feel matches your acts of faith.

Make the difference you were made for, daring to trust in an outcome you can't yet see. When you do, amazing things will happen, things you'll miss if you give up too soon.

You were created with purpose, and you are meant to fulfill that purpose. Do not grow weary in doing what you are made to do. Take a deep breath and make that fresh start — you have the unique opportunity to live a life of meaning, precisely where you are. If not you, then who will fill the void? Possibly no one.

We are all better off because you exist!

# Resources:

## Web Sites and Phone Numbers

EMS1
ems1.com

Cop Line
http://www.copline.org/
(800) 267 - 5463

The Badge of Life
http://www.badgeoflife.com/

Safe Call Now
https://www.safecallnow.org/
(206)-459-3020

National Suicide Prevention Lifeline
https://suicidepreventionlifeline.org/
800-273-8255

Firefighter Behavioral Health Alliance
http://www.ffbha.org/

U.S. Fire Administration
https://www.usfa.fema.gov/current_events/010517.html

NAEMT
https://www.naemt.org/initiatives/ems-mental-health

Code Green Campaign
http://codegreencampaign.org/

*The Firefighter Training Podcast*
www.petelamb.com

*Within the Trenches Podcast*
#IAM911 movement

## Articles of Interest

https://adaa.org/understanding-anxiety/posttraumatic-stress-disorder-ptsd/symptoms

https://www.ptsd.va.gov/public/ptsd-overview/basics/symptoms_of_ptsd.asp

https://www.webmd.com/mental-health/tc/post-traumatic-stress-disorder--symptoms#2

http://www.emsworld.com/article/12009260/suicide-stress-and-ptsd-among-emergency-personnel

Footnote:
https://www.harleytherapy.co.uk/counselling/boosting-your-mood-volunteer.htm

## Podcasts

*Within the Trenches*

*Fire Fighter Training*

*True Murder*

*CoronerTalk*

*Tending Your Dreams*

## Books

*Police Suicide: Is Police Culture Killing Our Officers?* 1st Edition by Dr. Ron Rufo 2015

*Police Suicide: Acuity of Influence* by Michael J. Alicea 2015

*Police Suicide: Risk Factors and Intervention Measures* 1st Edition 2017
by Richard Armitage, PhD

*Getting Through What You Can't Get Over* by Anita Agers Brooks 2015

*The Worst is Over* by CCH, Judith Acosta LISW and Judith Simon Prager PhD

# About the Authors:

**Darren Dake, D-ABMDI , CI, CCI** is a national speaker, author, and the founder of the ***Death Investigation Training Academy*** (DITA), and ***Coroner Talk*™** ***podcast.*** He began his career in public service in 1986, when he joined the ranks of the United States Army Military Police. After serving for several years, he left military service as a Gulf War Veteran and began a life-long journey in civilian law enforcement.

Darren has worked in the capacity of jail/detention officer, street patrol, as a detective sergeant and then lieutenant commander of a criminal investigation division. Throughout the past twenty years, Darren has also served as an investigator for the coroner's office in his county, and after retiring from full-time law enforcement, he continued to work as a Coroner/MDI investigator. Darren is a certified instructor for the Law Enforcement Learning Center and American Board of Medicolegal Death Investigators (ABMDI).

**Darren Dake, D-ABMDI , CI, CCI**
**ditacademy.org**
Retired law enforcement officer, present-day coroner
Founder of the ***Death Investigation Training Academy*** and the ***Coroner Talk podcast***

********

**Anita Agers Brooks, CPT, CLTF, CCS,** motivates 21st century women and men to dynamic break-throughs, blending mind, heart, body, and spirit, as an Inspirational Business/Life Coach, International Speaker, Certified Personality Trainer, and Common Trauma Expert. Tune into her podcast, ***Tending Your Dreams***, beginning March 2018.

A multi-published, award-winning author, Anita's titles reach a wide range of audiences in the Christian and general marketplaces. Her books include the Amazon Best Seller and Readers' Favorite International Award Winner, ***Getting Through What You Can't Get Over***, Barbour Publishing. Her next book, ***Exceedingly: Stories, Skills, and Strategies for Unearthing Your Abundant Purpose***, releases in 2019 with Kregel Publishing. You can find her titles at most bookstores and online retailers.

Anita fulfills her mission to help people make fresh starts with fresh faith, sharing hope and healing from the page and the stage. Connect and keep up with Anita on social media or at anitabrooks.com. Email anita@anitabrooks.com for more information or to inquiries about having her speak to your group.

\*\*\*\*\*\*\*\*

88045405R00113